Little Bites

little bites

100 HEALTHY, KID-FRIENDLY SNACKS

Christine Chitnis and Sarah Waldman

PHOTOGRAPHS BY Christine Chitnis

ROOST BOOKS
BOSTON & LONDON / 2015

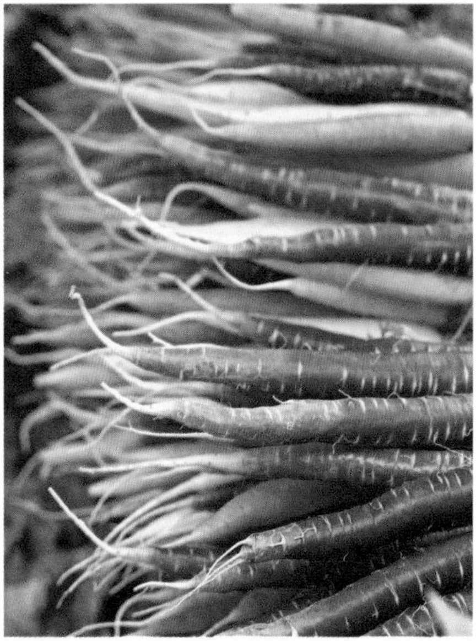

ROOST BOOKS
An imprint of Shambhala Publications, Inc.
Horticultural Hall
300 Massachusetts Avenue
Boston, Massachusetts 02115
roostbooks.com

9 8 7 6 5 4 3 2 1

First Edition
Printed in China

♾ This edition is printed on acid-free paper that meets the American National Standards Institute Z39.48 Standard.
♻ Shambhala makes every effort to print on recycled paper. For more information please visit www.shambhala.com.

Distributed in the United States by Penguin Random House LLC and in Canada by Random House of Canada Ltd

Designed by Daniel Urban-Brown

LIBRARY OF CONGRESS CATALOGING-IN-PUBLICATION DATA

Chitnis, Christine.
Little bites: 100 healthy, kid-friendly snacks /
Christine Chitnis and Sarah Waldman;
photographs by Christine Chitnis.—First edition.
pages cm
Includes bibliographical references and index.
ISBN 978-1-61180-177-4
1. Snack foods. 2. Children—Nutrition. I. Waldman, Sarah.
II. Title.
TX740.C43 2015
641.5'3—dc23
2014022055

FOR ALL FAMILIES, THAT YOUR KITCHEN MAY BE THE HEART OF YOUR HOME.

Contents

Preface / ix
Introduction / 1

COOKING WITH SEASONAL AND LOCAL INGREDIENTS / 5
THE FAMILY KITCHEN / 13
ON THE GO / 21
THE FAMILY PANTRY / 27

THE RECIPES / 37
SPRING / 39
SUMMER / 97
FALL / 151
WINTER / 207

Acknowledgments / 262
Resources / 264
Recipes by Category / 268
Index / 271
About Us / 278

Preface

SARAH AND I MET AT OUR LOCAL BAKERY when our sons were no more than a few weeks old, a fitting location given our food-centered friendship. Despite both of us being in a new-mom fog, we quickly bonded over our love of fresh, seasonal, wholesome cooking, as well as our passion for writing and photography. After that fateful meeting, we planned many a day trip with our boys, and the pretrip conversation inevitably turned to food—specifically what to pack for snack time. As our boys grew older, it seemed they couldn't go more than ten minutes without needing a little something to munch! Sarah and I agreed that the snacks didn't need to be junk food—the crackers, sugary treats, and other foods that we think of as snacks. In fact, we both believe that snack time provides an ideal opportunity to squeeze nutritionally dense, wholesomely delicious foods into our children's diets in exciting and inventive ways. *Little Bites* was born out of our shared experience as on-the-go, health-conscious moms focused on preparing food for our growing—and expanding—families. We're in the thick of it, with toddlers and babies needing every ounce of our attention, so we understand the need for simplicity and efficiency when it comes to feeding our crew.

Our goal is to offer recipes for simple, wholesome food made from ingredients that everyone can recognize and attain. We are not interested in being fancy, because quite frankly all of us busy parents haven't got the time. We believe in using the freshest, highest-quality ingredients possible—

whether from our gardens, the farmers' market, our local farms, or the grocery store—and letting those ingredients speak for themselves. We hope to instill in our children a love of simple, delicious, healthy food, and to give them the skills to make good food choices in the crazy food culture in which we live.

For *Little Bites,* Sarah brought to the table a background in nutrition and her unbelievable skill for developing fresh, original, and interesting recipes. Her flavor pairings are at once familiar and surprising to the palate, and as a mother she cooks naturally with little ones in mind. While Sarah handled things in the kitchen, my job was to bring to life the flavor and beauty of the seasons through my writing and photography. As with any labor of love, we relied on the many helping hands of friends and family to bring this book into being. It was a true group effort, and for that we are so thankful.

During the early stages of this book I described the concept to a friend, and—to my surprise—a look of horror crossed her face. "You mean now I have to find time to cook snacks in addition to three meals every day?" On the contrary, our intention is to show how with a bit of planning making healthy snacks from scratch can easily fit into your busy life. With proper packing and storing, a Sunday afternoon cooking spree can set you up for a week's worth of wholesome snacking, and these recipes also make wonderful breakfasts, lunches, and dinner sides. I hope that many become beloved additions to your family's meal repertoire.

We're all busy. The fact of the matter is that kids keep us on our toes. From the morning school rush to the afternoon sports shuffle, from endless hours spent at the playground to leisurely summer days at the shore, I hope our snack recipes will inspire you to take along foods that will nourish your entire family, one bite at a time.

Introduction

ANYONE WITH CHILDREN KNOWS the stampede that occurs whenever the phrase "snack time" is announced. Children think of snacks as fun, tasty, easy-to-eat foods, but we parents know the very best snacks are all that and more: when done right, snacks give our kids a needed boost of energy, whether after a long day of school or during an especially active trip to the playground, and they deliver dense amounts of nutrition in a small package. The best way to provide your kids with great snacks—treats that are economical as well as healthy and delicious—is to make them yourself.

Making your own snacks may seem overwhelming—after all, the whole idea of snacks is that they're easy!—but thinking of snack food as only prepackaged foods you can quickly grab from a box or bag has its consequences. Fast food, packaged snacks, and highly processed treats can have a negative impact on our health, and especially the health of growing children. Snacks you prepare yourself from high-quality ingredients will be healthier, tastier, and better for everyone.

Sarah and I invite our boys to join us in the kitchen to sift, measure, roll, and knead alongside us when we cook. It is important to us that our sons understand the entire process of how our meals end up on the table—from the hands that grew and harvested our ingredients to the hands that cooked them. These homemade snacks are so quick and easy, they are a good way to shift toward kitchen-based recreation; eventually you'll have carved out more food-focused time in your family's life for things like seasonal celebratory meals. As our lives have become busier, the art of cooking is being lost. We have forgotten what it means to seek out high-quality ingredients, gather in the kitchen, and cook together with intention and joy. I hope our recipes put that joy back into your cooking experience.

The snacks here were created with busy families in mind: the recipes are straightforward, and although a few ingredients may be new to you, most are old friends and easy to find. Sarah and I firmly believe in using "real" ingredients: real cream, real butter, real sugar—you get the picture! We're not into substitutes and ingredients we can't pronounce. Of course, some whole-food ingredients are healthier than others, and we don't suggest you snack on a bar of butter rolled in sugar. Our motto is "everything in moderation." Our kids enjoy sweet treats such as our recipes for Lemon-Glazed Blueberry Donuts, Dark-Chocolate-Dipped Coconut Macaroons, and Sesame Seed Candy—but even these goodies contain ingredients that have beneficial health properties for children's growing bodies: fruits, vegetables, nuts, seeds, whole grains, and healthy fats.

We're also not fans of disguising food to get children to eat it. Sarah and I want our boys to

know what spinach looks like, how it grows, and how it tastes. We try to find ways to make all foods appealing; if we don't succeed, we'll try preparing it in a different way, keeping in mind that sometimes there will be flavors that just don't appeal to a specific palate. And that is okay. Luckily, nature provides us with an overflowing arsenal of flavors, textures, and colors. Each season brings with it an abundant and unique harvest, perfectly equipped to supply our bodies with the vitamins and nutrients needed for that particular time of year. By teaching our children to eat in-tune with the seasons we ensure their bodies are fueled with optimum nutrition.

Although our snacks were created with children in mind, they can be enjoyed by the whole family. My husband can attest to that fact, as he often wolfed down whatever recipe I was testing before my boys even had a chance to taste. Of course, this was frustrating at times, but it also gave me immense satisfaction to know that our creations are pleasing to palates of all ages. We've even included ways to adapt these recipes for babies who are just beginning their journey with solid foods.

In addition to one hundred recipes, we've included a wealth of information on food planning, shopping locally, packaging snacks in a healthy, sustainable way, and the nutritional benefits of the ingredients we use. Keeping in mind that this is a cookbook for on-the-go families, we've kept the information concise. We'd love for you to read every word, but more important, we want you to get cooking! It is our sincere hope that *Little Bites* will become a staple in your kitchen, helping you to leave the packaged snacks behind and moving you toward an active family life filled with wholesome, seasonal, energy-boosting snacks.

Cooking with Seasonal and Local Ingredients

CHILDREN ARE BORN WITH AN INNATE SENSE OF SEASONALITY. IN THE SUMMER MONTHS, I NOTICE THAT MY BOYS NATURALLY STAY UP LATER, SLEEP IN, CRAVE LIGHTER FOODS, AND HAVE A DESIRE TO SPEND EVERY WAKING MOMENT OUTDOORS. WHEN THE COLDER weather comes creeping in, they begin to shift to earlier bedtimes, and their food choices tend toward dishes that offer warmth and comfort. They want to play indoors, snuggle under piles of blankets with stacks of books, and take long hot baths before bedtime. Although we still make it outside to take crisp fall walks and, later, build snow forts, we slow our pace and retreat indoors for much of the day. Without a mention of the word *spring*, they begin feeling the pull once again to play outside, they chase the light with later bedtimes, and the cycle continues.

Somewhere along the way, after we've slipped past childhood and taken on the distractions of adulthood, we lose our natural connection to the seasons. We get stuck in food ruts without considering that the changing calendar might call for different recipes and ingredient choices. However, if we're able to tap back into the natural rhythm of the seasons, we'll find that the earth provides our bodies with exactly what they need to stay healthy and thrive. During the warm months, berries, peaches, watermelon, and tomatoes supply us with the base for light, refreshing, hydrating meals. Sweet potatoes, beets, squash, and kale provide us with the heartiness and warmth that we crave during the colder months, not to mention the vitamins and nutrients needed to stave off colds and flus.

Foods just taste better when they are at their peak of ripeness. Have you ever eaten a grocery-store strawberry in January? You probably found it to be flavorless, colorless, and hard—simply no comparison to a farmers' market strawberry picked at the height of spring, still warm from the sun. A local, in-season strawberry is smaller, its color rich, its flesh tender and juicy and packed with flavor.

Produce harvested and consumed during its natural growing season has been proven to be better nutritionally. If produce is picked prematurely, before it has had time to ripen, it never reaches its full nutritional potential. Such is the case for those out-of-season strawberries picked before maturity, wrapped in plastic, shipped across the continent, and left to redden on the shelves. Independent farmers wait until their produce is perfectly ripe before bringing it to market, often having picked it that very morning. Allowing produce to ripen naturally increases the plant's amount of phytonutrients, and as a crop gets closer to full ripeness, it converts its phytonutrients to the most readily absorbable forms, which keep your body working properly and help prevent disease. That's scientific talk meaning higher concentrations of healthy stuff for you and your kids! And because fruits and vegetables begin losing nutrients after they've been picked, the less they sit around, the better.

But if the flavor and nutritional content aren't enough to convince you of the merits of in-season eating, consider for a moment the environmental benefits. That January strawberry, for example—how far did it have to travel to reach you? Perhaps it was shipped from Florida or imported from South America and traveled long distances by plane, truck, train, or ship—or a combination—to reach your plate. All of those methods consume energy and contribute to air pollution and unhealthy air quality. Additionally, the money you spend to purchase that imported food does not stay in your local economy. Buying locally contributes to efficient and less-polluting distribution structures and supports healthy communities and a strong local economy.

The idea of in-season eating is not just a trend. It is a concept that has existed for most of human history, when the only choice was to eat what each season provided. Of course, Sarah and I are nowhere near perfect on this front, and we're not suggesting absolutism as a goal. We still purchase bananas, which will never be a seasonal or local fruit for us New Englanders. And we would never deny our kids a stack of blueberry pancakes at their favorite breakfast joint, even in the dead of winter. Our goal is simply to bring more seasonal awareness to the table. Although our boys miss raspberries and peaches during the winter months, they look forward to their reappearance with much excitement. In an age of instant gratification, there is such beauty in the slow turn of the earth, and the gentle reappearance of each season.

SHOP LOCAL

One of the wonderful benefits of eating in season is that it requires locally produced foods. Although large grocery stores offer the convenience of one-stop shopping, they are often lacking when it comes to locally sourced, seasonal produce. We greatly applaud the efforts of small markets, grocers, and co-ops that stock local food products and work with farms to supply their customers with local produce. The options for sourcing local food continue to grow as consumers take a greater interest in their food choices.

If you're not familiar with the farms and food producers in your area, I suggest this fun exercise: on a map, draw a circle with a thirty- to fifty-mile radius, with your home at the center. Get online and research every orchard, farm stand, beekeeper, dairy farmer, maple syrup operation, meat farmer, farmers' market, and food vendor in the towns within that circle. If you are lucky enough to live in an area where there is an active local food scene, a map like this may already exist. Let this map be your guide as you work your way through our recipes. It may feel like quite a bit of work at first, but look at your map as an adventure waiting to happen: take your kids along as you explore the local food offerings in your area.

Children love farms and farmers' markets; both venues appeal to their natural curiosity. U-pick options are usually enjoyable for kids, who love the task of filling their baskets full of berries, peaches, or apples. Many farms encourage exploring, and kids might be allowed to visit the chicken coop to search for eggs or watch the farmer feed a slop bucket to the pigs. Farmers' markets offer a wealth of experiences for children. Ask them to help you with your shopping, giving them the independence to find the best sweet corn vendor or sweetest peach grower. Most vendors will offer little samples of their goods so shoppers can experience their quality firsthand. Kids will enjoy feasting on the prepared food offerings also, whether from a local ice cream vendor or wood-oven pizza maker. Many farmers' markets even offer entertainment for kids, such as local music, crafts, or a story time. Plan to make a morning out of celebrating your local food scene and all it has to offer.

Sourcing foods locally doesn't need to burden your food budget. It is a widely spread misconception that eating healthy, local food costs more, but with a bit of planning and research, you can save money when buying fresh, wholesome ingredients and preparing food from scratch. It's worth remembering, too, that there is much more to the cost of food than simply the dollar amount. When you consider the true cost of imported, packaged foods—the cost to the environment, the cost to our health, and the cost to the local economy—eating locally sourced foods feels like an investment in our future. Of course, we all do our best to find a balance between our budgets and our ideals. Here are our top six money-saving tips for buying high-quality food.

1. BUY IN BULK. Whether you are buying bulk almonds and rolled oats at your local health food store or buying strawberries by the bushel at your local farm stand, there are hefty savings to be had when you buy large quantities. Test this advice by comparing the price and weight of that bushel of farm-fresh strawberries with the price and weight of a small plastic container of strawberries from the grocery store. The savings will be evident.

2. JOIN A CSA. Community-supported agriculture is a model that allows consumers to buy a share of the farm's crops for a given season. Each week, shareholders are given a large box of in-season produce. For a one-time investment, you'll be able to count on a season's worth of local, just-harvested produce. Compare prices of CSAs in your area, and ask farmers what you can expect in each box; you won't have to spend a nickel on grocery-store produce if you invest wisely in a CSA. (And some CSAs offer dairy and meat in addition to fruits and vegetables.)

3. PRESERVE IN-SEASON PRODUCE. Buying and freezing several bushels of blueberries in season will save you from buying either expensive imported blueberries or the packaged frozen variety during the off-season. With the cost of those small bags of organic frozen blueberries, making smoothies year-round would be pretty costly. However, with a bit of planning and preparing during the height of each harvest, you will have a freezer and pantry full of berries and other produce that was purchased when the price was lowest and the quality was highest.

4. LEARN THE LINGO. So many of the labels slapped on our foods are merely marketing ploys. Phrases like "all natural" and "whole foods" have no legal meaning, and their use in labeling is not regulated, yet you may end up paying more simply for the illusion of healthier food. The term *organic* involves the most specific criteria. As defined by the USDA, organic meat, poultry, eggs, and dairy products come from animals that are given no antibiotics or growth hormones. Organic plant foods are produced without the use of most conventional pesticides, fertilizers made with synthetic ingredients or sewage sludge, bioengineering, or ionizing radiation.

5. GROW YOUR OWN. Growing a few pots of herbs or tending a small bed of vegetables can help to offset the costs of more expensive produce. I am always amazed at the cost of a few basil leaves or branches of thyme at our chain grocery store. If you are someone who enjoys cooking with herbs, a few small potted plants can keep you in supply all year long. I keep basil, rosemary, thyme, and mint growing in pots outdoors throughout the spring, summer, and fall seasons, and before the first frost hits, I find them a sunny windowsill to call home during the winter months. If you are interested in growing a few vegetables, you could easily keep your entire family supplied with tomatoes, carrots, radishes, lettuce, kale, spinach, and other bountiful plants by tending a 6-by-9-foot raised bed.

6. FOCUS ON THE DIRTY DOZEN AND THE CLEAN FIFTEEN. At a grocery store, you will find organic produce is more costly than its conventionally grown counterparts. By focusing on the "Dirty Dozen" and the "Clean Fifteen" (as identified by the Environmental Working Group, see the following lists) you can make the most of your grocery budget. The Dirty Dozen are the U.S. produce items that contain the most chemicals after being conventionally grown. The Clean Fifteen are the conventionally grown U.S. produce items that contain the least chemical contamination. Strive to purchase organic versions of the produce listed in "The Dirty Dozen," and worry less about those in "The Clean Fifteen." Although these lists apply to national-scale producers, they can still be helpful information to keep in mind when shopping locally, where you have the benefit of being able to ask local farmers what chemicals they have used. For example, a local, conventional farmer near me grows a classic Dirty Dozen crop—strawberries—but as a small-scale farmer she actually uses fewer chemicals on her strawberries than national-level growers are using on their Clean Fifteen crops.

The Dirty Dozen

APPLES

CELERY

CHERRY TOMATOES

CUCUMBERS

GRAPES

NECTARINES, IMPORTED

PEACHES

POTATOES

SNAP PEAS, IMPORTED

SPINACH

STRAWBERRIES

SWEET BELL PEPPERS

Plus:

HOT PEPPERS

KALE/COLLARDS

The Clean Fifteen

ASPARAGUS

AVOCADOS

CABBAGE

CANTALOUPE

CAULIFLOWER

EGGPLANT

GRAPEFRUITS

KIWIFRUITS

MANGOES

ONIONS

PAPAYAS

PINEAPPLES

SWEET CORN

SWEET PEAS, FROZEN

SWEET POTATOES

The Family Kitchen

THE KITCHEN IS TRULY THE HEART OF OUR HOMES, WHERE WE SPEND TIME MAKING AND CELEBRATING FOOD THROUGHOUT EACH OF THE SEASONS. RUNNING AN EFFICIENT FAMILY KITCHEN IS NO SMALL TASK. IT TAKES PLANNING, ORGANIZATION, AND, WHEN KIDS ARE involved, a sense of humor and endless patience. Sarah and I have compiled a list of tips and tricks that help our kitchens run more smoothly, including strategies for food planning, time-saving cooking techniques, and a few of our favorite kitchen appliances. The kitchen should be a place where all members of the family feel welcome to join in and get cooking, so we've also put together a few ideas for getting kids involved.

STRATEGIES FOR FOOD PLANNING

Coordinating an active family life requires organization: calendars, family meetings, and various other tactics ensure life runs smoothly. When the same approach is taken to the family kitchen, the cooking process becomes easier and more enjoyable. Planning and preparation are a home chef's two best friends!

MENU PLAN AS A FAMILY. Sit down together and make a menu plan for the week, including breakfasts, lunches, dinners, and—of course—snacks. Make a one-week template with daily slots for

each meal, and invite the kids to weigh in with their favorite meal and snack choices. Once the list is complete it will provide a helpful outline for the week's grocery list. Keeping a notebook of family favorites can help streamline the process, and bringing new cookbooks, food magazines, and online recipes to the weekly meeting will keep things fresh and exciting. Family menu planning can be a venue for important nutritional discussions, as well, and also spur ideas for fun family activities. For example, if your menu plan includes our Blueberry Baked Oatmeal Cups (page 110), a visit to the pick-your-own berry farm might be in order!

PLAN YOUR SHOPPING. Keep an ongoing shopping list tacked to the refrigerator. Throughout the week add items that you need, and once you plan your weekly meals, add your recipe ingredients. Keep a separate list for the farmers' market to avoid double purchases. Aim for one large weekly shopping trip per week, as well as one visit to the farmers' market for fresh, local produce and food products. Build in enough time to thoroughly unpack after shopping: transfer dry goods to airtight

glass storage jars and store produce in a way that will prolong its freshness (see tips in Prepare Produce, page 16).

COOK AHEAD. Plan a few cooking sessions separate from mealtime cooking throughout the week, whether it be on the weekend, a weeknight after the kids are in bed, or during the day when the kids are in school. Anything that can be made ahead can be slotted for this time, as well as snacks and meal staples that store well. Sarah always makes a big pot of brown rice on Sunday for quick lunches and dinners throughout the beginning of the week. I like to make and freeze dough for cookies, muffins, pizza, and other baked goods during my Sunday cooking time. This allows me to hit the ground running on Monday morning.

ORGANIZATION IS KEY. Keep your older children's favorite cups, dishes, snack containers, and utensils organized in a low, easy-to-reach drawer so they can help themselves and assist in packing their own snacks. This also applies to favorite foods. The lowest shelf of the refrigerator is a perfect place for keeping containers of precut vegetables and fruits, mason jars of prepared smoothies, and other kid-friendly snacks. Keeping jars of dried fruit, nuts, and other pantry snacks in a handy location will encourage older kids to help themselves to healthy pick-me-ups. Do a similar thing for baby: set aside a specific area in the refrigerator and pantry for baby-friendly foods. When preparing a recipe add a portion to baby's stash, eliminating the need to cook separate meals for the little one. For example, when making Sweet Potato–Cornmeal Muffins (page 240), reserve a cup of mashed sweet potato for baby before adding the rest to the batter. Our Baby Friendly call-outs in each recipe suggest what can be set aside for baby.

BUILD A FAMILY PANTRY. Having well-organized supplies on hand for creating favorite snacks will make both spontaneous and planned cooking projects simple and stress-free. Keep large glass storage jars of baking supplies, grains, rolled oats, rice, nuts, and dried fruits well stocked at all times. See Pantry Staples (page 28) for a detailed list of what a well-stocked pantry might contain.

TIME-SAVING COOKING TECHNIQUES

In a dream world, we'd have time to savor the cooking process. While there are in fact times when cooking can be a relaxing and inspiring task, the daily reality of cooking for a family usually falls a bit more on the frantic side of the spectrum. Our time-saving techniques will help you to make the most of your cooking time, so that even a five-minute mad dash into the kitchen can allow you to get something healthy cooking.

SAY OKAY TO SOME CANNED/PACKAGED GOODS. Certain foods just make sense to buy canned or prepackaged to save time and money. Things like beans, chickpeas, crushed tomatoes, and broths are time consuming to make and can be purchased at a high quality and low price.

PREPARE PRODUCE. When you come home from the market, wash and chop produce so it is ready and waiting for you. Wrap washed greens in a damp paper towel, and store in a mesh produce bag. Store chopped produce in lidded glass containers to preserve freshness. Keep in mind that some whole fruits and vegetables should not be refrigerated, including tomatoes, avocados, potatoes, onions, thick-skinned produce such as melons and squashes, stone fruits, and bananas. Pick over your berries for mold as soon as you bring them home. Mold spreads like wildfire among berries, so even one moldy berry can quickly infect the whole bunch. Don't wash berries until you are ready to use them. Herbs such as basil, mint, rosemary, and chives should be stored upright in a glass cup or jar with fresh cold water in the bottom. Think of it as an herb bouquet and freshen the water daily. Taking the time to properly store produce will ensure optimum freshness and longevity.

GET A HEAD START. If a recipe calls for an item with a long cooking time, begin preparing it when you have a free moment. Throw a pot of grains or beans on the stove while you unpack your groceries. Roast a pan of vegetables, a few sweet potatoes, or half a pumpkin while you are waiting for your kids to get home from school. Preparing time-consuming recipe items ahead of schedule will really pay off when you are cooking for a hungry, eager crowd.

SHARE WITH FRIENDS. Organize a swap of homegrown and wholesome items with a few friends. Bake a couple loaves of bread in exchange for backyard eggs or produce from a home garden. You might even invite a few friends over for a cooking date. Ask each friend to bring a favorite recipe, along with enough ingredients for everyone to make it. You can divide the recipes among the group or work together on each recipe. Not only does cooking with friends make the process much more enjoyable; it also saves time and money, and everyone goes home with a variety of new meals and snacks to try.

INVOLVING KIDS IN PREPARATION, COOKING, AND EATING

Kids love to help in the kitchen, and although that sometimes means flour-strewn countertops and sticky fingers, it's worth the mess. When the kitchen becomes a place where all are welcome to help, an attitude of curiosity, engagement, and enthusiasm builds around food choices.

SAY YES TO EAGER KITCHEN HELPERS. Steer kids toward tasks that are safe and appropriate for their age, such as washing produce, snapping apart vegetables such as green beans and broccoli spears, tearing up leafy greens, measuring and stirring ingredients, holding the electric beater, sprinkling in herbs and seasonings, kneading bread, rolling out pastry or cookie dough, and setting the timer. Stock up on a few fun tools that are safe for children to use in the kitchen and that fit their smaller hands, including kid-safe knives, smaller bowls, and child-size mixing spoons, whisks, and aprons. Your little ones will feel extra important with their own equipment.

LET THEM EXPERIMENT. Making concoctions out of inexpensive items is a great way to get kids excited about cooking, allowing them to feel empowered in the kitchen without the stress of following a recipe. My boys have a play kitchen in our real kitchen, and often I'll fill their toy pots and pans with a handful of dried beans, a bit of flour, and some discarded vegetable peels, and they'll "cook" dinner for me while I cook beside them.

HAVE FUN WITH FOOD. Nothing is sillier than playing with your food! After a productive trip to the farmers' market, stage a taste test between different apple varieties, or whip up a batch of our Oven-Baked French Fries (page 224) made from various colors of potatoes and see what your kids think of a purple french fry. Keep kids excited about eating by mixing things up. Eat outside, have a picnic in the living room, read a book together while snacking, serve small snacks with toothpicks to poke and grab. Having fun with food leads to an open mind when it comes to new flavors, textures, and colors.

RELAX. Look at the big picture of your child's diet—what they've eaten over a week, month, or even season rather than a day at a time. Don't get stressed if they refuse to try new foods, or show no interest in helping in the kitchen. A relaxed attitude when it comes to eating helps kids foster a healthy relationship with food. Always ask your children if they would like a bite, and use positive encouragement around the issue. Never threaten or force foods, and let go of the idea of the "Clean Plate Club." Children can sense when they are full, and forcing them to clean their plate only teaches them to override their natural hunger signals.

LEAD BY EXAMPLE. Kids will be more open to trying new foods if they see their parents, siblings, and friends doing the same. Be willing to try everything once, even if it's just for the sake of your kids, and steer clear of passing your own food prejudices on to your kids. I can't stand olives, and I assumed that meant my boys wouldn't like them either. When a friend offered an appetizer platter of olives, I was shocked to find my little guys eagerly digging in. It turns out they love olives. Lesson learned: every single person has a distinct palate. Allow your children to cultivate their own unique sense of taste.

KITCHEN APPLIANCES AND SUPPLIES

Every family has their favorite kitchen tools, but here are a few special tools that we highly recommend for their ease, efficiency, and results.

CAST IRON SKILLET. Cast iron is a great alternative to nonstick pans, which contain harmful chemicals in their coatings. Season a new iron skillet with oil to make your own heavy-duty nonstick pan perfect for cooking pancakes, fritters, eggs, and more. It's an excellent investment, because a well-tended cast iron pan can last a lifetime. In fact, you can often find amazing cast iron skillets at your local thrift shop for a steal.

FOOD PROCESSOR. This multiuse tool makes pastry dough, shreds vegetables, whizzes soft fillings for turnovers and dumplings, and quickly combines ingredients for dips such as pesto and hummus.

ICE CREAM MAKER. Sarah usually steers away from one-trick tools, but a basic ice cream maker churns out her son's all-time favorite dessert with ease, and it is a great investment for your kid-friendly kitchen. Making your own ice cream and frozen yogurt with seasonal produce, organic dairy, and natural sweeteners allows you to indulge your kids all year long.

BLENDER. A high-quality blender is a wise investment if you are a family that loves smoothies, dips, soups, sauces, and nut milks. Look for a trusted brand, as the cheaper models may have trouble with the tougher stuff, such as frozen fruits, ice, and nuts.

On the Go

LET'S BE HONEST, WE ALL EAT ON THE GO. AS MUCH AS I'D LOVE TO SIT AROUND THE TABLE AS A FAMILY FOR THREE SQUARE MEALS A DAY, THAT IS JUST NOT THE REALITY OF MY LIFE WITH KIDS. I AM A STICKLER FOR A SEATED FAMILY DINNER, BUT WHEN IT COMES to eating at other times during the day, I have come to peace with the fact that it may happen in the stroller, walking to school, at the playground, or in the car. And that's okay as long as the food we're eating is nourishing, wholesome, and packed up in a healthy way that reduces waste.

Inevitably, it seems, packing and storing food involves a lot of plastic. Although plastic products are very convenient, we strongly recommend avoiding them as much as possible. Most plastic products, from plastic wrap and plastic bags to baby bottles and sippy cups, leach hormone-like chemicals, even prior to being exposed to real-world conditions such as sunlight, heat, microwaves, and dishwashers. And guess where those chemicals end up? In whatever food is being stored in the plastic container. Some of these chemicals act like estrogen, the sex hormone, in the body, and they occur even in the "better" plastic products labeled "BPA-free." In addition to these estrogen-like chemicals, other food-grade plastics do contain BPA, a developmental, neural, and reproductive toxin.

For this reason, I strive for a plastic-free kitchen, although I'm the first to admit that I am far from perfection on this count. Condiments, deli bags, cheese, baking ingredients—so many items we need come wrapped in plastic. Simply steer away from buying plastic-wrapped items whenever alternatives are available, but when it is unavoidable, I transfer products to safe containers as soon as possible. You can easily get into the habit of bringing your own organic muslin or cotton bags to the grocery store for produce and bulk items, eliminating the need for plastic bags. With a bit of planning and creativity, plastic can be avoided much of the time. That being said, you'll notice that almost all products on the market these days have at least a little bit of plastic—whether it is the lid of a glass snack container or the rim of glass storage jar. Don't panic. As a general rule of thumb, the less plastic the better.

HEALTHY ALTERNATIVES TO PLASTIC PACKAGING

The way in which you package food can be just as important as what and how you cook. After taking the time to source fresh ingredients and whip up a healthy treat, why stick it in a plastic container that could compromise its quality and safety? Here are our simple, affordable solutions for food storage and packing.

GLASS CONTAINERS AND JARS. Glass is the safest food-storage option. It's incredibly sustainable thanks to its long life and 100 percent recyclability. Glass is impermeable and nonporous, so it doesn't admit or hold on to contaminants; it goes from the freezer to the oven to the table and back again; and, contrary to what you might think, it can be very durable and hold up to many years of use. There are so many wonderful glass products on the market, from small glass snack containers with snap lids to retain freshness to Weck-brand jars for sealed-tight smoothies, dips, and sauces. Check out our Resources section for some of our favorite glass snack-storage products. Use your best judgment when allowing kids to handle breakable glass containers; however, kids who are introduced to breakable items early on often develop a quick understanding of how they should be handled.

My absolute favorite food storage containers are glass jars: mason jars, jelly jars, recycled condiment jars—I love them all. Cheap, effective, safe, and nice on the eyes, I use jars for storing bulk items, such as nuts, grains, pasta, dried beans, baking supplies, coffee beans, and dried fruit; for keeping refrigerated soups, stews, oatmeal, fruit salad, and leftovers; and for packing a wide variety of snacks. I've even been known to tote a mason jar of muffins to the playground. Look for jars that have a tight seal, which makes them perfect for storing liquids as well. Glass is easy to wash, and it won't harbor bacteria. My favorite jars are child-size mason jars with handles and tops that fit a straw—perfect for smoothies and fresh juices.

BEESWAX WRAP. For a safe, sustainable alternative to plastic wrap try beeswax wrap. It is made by coating cotton or muslin with beeswax, jojoba oil, and tree resin. The coating makes the fabric waterproof, airtight, flexible, and adhesive enough to behave like plastic wrap. The antibacterial properties of beeswax and jojoba oil help keep food fresh naturally and allow the wrap to be used again and again. Happily, beeswax wrap has replaced plastic wrap in my kitchen. It is great for covering bowls of food, packing sandwiches, replacing plastic deli bags, and wrapping cheese. My favorite sources are beeswrap.com and abeego.com. If you are feeling crafty, you can easily make your own beeswax wrap by searching out tutorials online.

ORGANIC FABRIC SNACK BAGS. Reusable fabric snack bags are a sustainable and healthy alternative to brown paper bags and plastic sandwich bags, and their various sizes and shapes make packing lunch a cinch. You can easily wash fabric bags in the dishwasher, which only increases their convenience. Look for certified food-safe fabrics. MightyNest (mightnest.com) is a great source of a variety of fabric snack- and sandwich-bag options. If you must use a disposable paper bag, choose a 100 percent unbleached variety.

STAINLESS STEEL CONTAINERS. Stainless steel is reusable, recyclable, durable, and free from leaching ingredients, so it is a great option for kid-friendly packaging. Stainless steel is an alloy composed of natural elements. It poses no health risks, contains no toxins, will not impart any peculiar taste or smell to stored food, and is practically indestructible. If cared for properly, stainless steel containers can last a lifetime. Several companies offer lunch-box-size containers with compartments for different food items and even reusable stainless steel straws. Our favorite sources for stainless steel containers are MightyNest (mightnest.com), LunchBots (lunchbots.com), and Wild Mint (wildmintshop.com), which all offer BPA-free, phthalate-free, and lead-free guarantees.

UNBLEACHED PARCHMENT PAPER. Parchment paper is coated in silicone and used for baking, steaming fish and vegetables, and general hot food preparation, while wax paper is coated in wax and designed to be used with chilled food items. Parchment paper is superior, as it can be used safely in the oven, microwave, freezer, and refrigerator. If you wipe it down, often it can be used repeatedly, whereas wax paper is generally a one-time-use product. Unbleached parchment paper is the safest choice.

ALUMINUM FOIL. Aluminum foil is costly to make and is resource intensive, but it can be used and recycled many times over. If we use it correctly and recycle it, aluminum foil is the product whose life span never ends. There have been studies that show trace amounts of aluminum can leach into stored foods, however, so use foil sparingly.

The Family Pantry

A WELL-STOCKED PANTRY IS THE KEY TO AN EFFICIENT KITCHEN. HAVING ABUNDANT DRY GOODS ON HAND MAKES BOTH PLANNED AND SPONTANEOUS BAKING PROJECTS ENJOYABLE AND STRESS FREE. THERE IS NOTHING WORSE THAN STARTING A RECIPE ONLY TO realize you're missing a key ingredient. A carefully planned pantry will also come to the rescue on those nights when your fridge is bare. A pot of beans or rice can provide the backbone for a healthy, quick meal with the addition of a few chopped veggies and a tempting sauce. Invest in large glass jars with airtight seals for storing grains, rice, beans, flours, sugars, and other pantry staples. Not only are glass jars safe, sustainable, and beautiful in their simplicity, but you can also see your ingredients, so you know when you're running low and need to restock. Most of the items we suggest can be bought in bulk at your local natural foods store as well as at select larger grocers.

FOOD INTOLERANCES AND ALLERGIES

Sarah and I are sensitive to the fact that every family has a unique set of challenges when it comes to dietary needs. In order to make sure there is something delicious for everyone, we have included recipes that are gluten free, nut free, and/or dairy free, and these are flagged with easy-to-spot icons. Nowadays, many schools are peanut and tree-nut free; while many of our recipes are already nut free, for others you can always skip the nuts or substitute seeds, which often provide a similar crunch. In recipes that call for nut butter, we recommend substituting sunflower seed butter to achieve the same creamy richness. We hope these icons point out that everyone in your family can enjoy healthful and delicious snacks, no matter what dietary restrictions they may face.

PANTRY STAPLES

Grains and Flours

The array of whole grains and flours available these days is overwhelming, but when you are armed with a bit of knowledge, the abundant options become exciting. Experiment with different flours for varied textures in your baking. Cornmeal adds crunch while almond meal imparts a nutty flavor; spelt flour packs a protein punch, and wheat germ can be added to baked goods and smoothies for a kick of fiber. If your family needs gluten-free options, you will occasionally have to play around with amounts to get the desired result.

ALMOND MEAL. Nut flours are different from nut meals only in that nuts are blanched when making flour, and some say this gives a more refined flavor. In our opinion, almond meal is just as good, and its advantage is that it can be made simply by giving almonds a whirl in a food processor. Full of protein and nutty in flavor, almond meal works well for baked goods, including our Lemon-Glazed Blueberry Donuts (page 148).

CORNMEAL. Gluten free and with a nice gritty heft, cornmeal imparts baked goods with a slight hint of rustic corn flavor. Great for baked goods, such as our Sweet Potato–Cornmeal Muffins (page 240), for making corn tortillas, or for coating tofu or chicken before cooking for a crunchy outer layer.

MILLET. A tiny gluten-free grain full of essential nutrients and rich in fiber and protein, millet binds together the ingredients of our Black Bean Cakes (page 136). This is a great grain to use in side dishes, heaped on top of a hearty salad, or as an alternative to rice or couscous.

QUINOA. Quinoa is a quick-cooking seed packed with essential amino acids, calcium, iron, and protein. This gluten-free grain is versatile and can be used in breakfast porridges, bean patties, and sweet desserts such as Quinoa Pudding with Raspberries and Pecans (page 84).

RICE. Brown, black, red, and wild rice are all chock-full of minerals, vitamins, antioxidants, and fiber—they're also tastier and more flavorful than white rice. The complete milling and polishing process that converts brown rice into white rice destroys most of the nutrients, leaving behind a nutritionally void, heavily processed product.

ROLLED OATS. While there are several oat options, including steel-cut oats and quick-cooking oats, we cast our vote for rolled oats, which fall right in the middle. Rolled oats are produced when whole grains of oats are steamed until soft and pliable, then pressed between rollers and dried. The resulting oats cook quickly, have a plethora of health benefits, and are great for using in oatmeal and baked goods, like our Blueberry Baked Oatmeal Cups (page 110). While rolled oats often have traces of gluten, Bob's Red Mill offers an outstanding gluten-free product.

SPELT FLOUR. Milled from spelt, this flour has more fiber and protein and less gluten (although it's not gluten free) than wheat. With a mild, slightly nutty flavor, this flour lends itself well to baking, especially in our Rhubarb-Lemon Biscotti (page 94).

UNBLEACHED ALL-PURPOSE FLOUR. Although it's not exactly a standout from a health perspective, there are moments in baking when you simply need an all-purpose flour. Ideal for baking bread and pizza dough, all-purpose flour has a neutral taste. We suggest always choosing flour labeled "unbleached," as most all-purpose flour has been treated with bleaching compounds, usually either benzoyl peroxide or some type of chlorine (yes, the strong stuff used to whiten clothes!).

WHEAT GERM. Wheat germ, the most nutritionally rich part of the wheat kernel, is packed with fiber, folate, healthy fatty acids, vitamin E, and minerals including iron, zinc, magnesium, calcium, selenium, and manganese. You can use it in baked goods, such as our Raspberry-Lemon Whole Wheat Mini Pancakes (page 134), or sprinkled into smoothies and over oatmeal and yogurt.

WHOLE WHEAT FLOUR. All-purpose, or white, flour is made from heavily refined and processed wheat grains, while whole wheat flour is made from grains that have been minimally processed. Therefore, the nutritional value of whole wheat flour is much higher, namely in fiber and vitamin content. Whole wheat flour will make your baked products denser and heavier than all-purpose flour. For a finer, silkier flour that produces light and fluffy baked goods, whole wheat "pastry" flour is best.

Sweeteners

It's no secret that most children have a sweet tooth. Instead of making sweets off-limits, why not create wholesome treats together at home using natural sweeteners? A well-stocked pantry should contain an array of sweeteners ranging from local maple syrup for topping oatmeal to coconut sugar for baking to whole dried dates for adding sweetness to smoothies.

We suggest starting babies off with naturally sweet foods and don't recommend introducing concentrated sweeteners until a year of age, if not later. Babies have not developed a taste for overly sweet food, so there is absolutely no reason to add sugar or other sweeteners to their food. Instead, using sweet fruits and vegetables and dried fruits is a great way to offer natural sweetness to a baby's palate. Mashed bananas, applesauce, dates, and sweet potatoes are just a few of the very sweet and healthful natural choices available.

AGAVE NECTAR (ALSO KNOWN AS AGAVE SYRUP). A sweetener produced from the agave plant, this syrup has a lower glycemic index than do most sugars and honey, meaning it does not cause a dramatic spike in blood sugar. It dissolves well in liquid, which makes it an ideal sweetener for our Raspberry Lemonade (page 120). However, keep in mind that agave nectar is extremely sweet, so use it sparingly in baked goods and porridges.

BROWN SUGAR. Brown sugar is pure cane sugar that contains a small amount of molasses. The molasses gives it a richer, deeper flavor than white sugar and also makes for a moister product that lends itself well to baking. Dark brown sugar has a strong molasses flavor, while light brown sugar has a milder flavor and a drier texture.

COCONUT SUGAR. A granulated sugar produced from the sap of cut flower buds of the coconut palm, coconut sugar has a lower glycemic index than refined white and brown sugar and can replace traditional sugar in all cooking and baked goods. It has a deep, rich, caramel flavor.

DATE SUGAR. A granulated sweetener made from dehydrated ground dates, date sugar has a rich, fruity flavor that is a perfect replacement for white sugar in many recipes. All the nutrients in the dates are still in the sugar, along with all their fiber.

DRIED FRUIT. A natural source of sweetness, dried fruit is great for snacking, adding to baked goods, topping oatmeal, and sweetening smoothies. Dates are a favorite for blending into smoothies, while dried cherries, raisins, cranberries, and apricots pair well with nuts and dark chocolate chunks for a quick, sweet-tooth-satisfying snack, such as our Jewel Mix (page 227). When using dried fruits as a sweetener, first soften them in hot water and then give them a quick whirl in the blender. This will produce a sweet, easy-to-use puree.

HONEY. A natural sweetener that contains antioxidants, vitamins, and minerals, honey is perfect for baking, sweetening smoothies, and drizzling over oatmeal. Raw unpasteurized honey, which hasn't been heated, contains many more health benefits, but be aware that honey contains bacteria that can damage infants' immature digestive systems. Hold off serving honey to your child until at least one year of age, and speak to your pediatrician before introducing honey (especially raw honey) into your baby's diet. Finding a source for local honey is easy, and it's worth the effort because commercially produced honey is often stripped of many of its health benefits during the pasteurization process.

PURE CANE SUGAR. Processed by crushing sugarcane until its sweet juice is released, then evaporating the water from the juice to create a concentrated crumble, pure cane sugar, which is light brown in color, is a better choice than refined white sugar, which undergoes extensive chemical processing before appearing on shelves. Although there are no health benefits to pure cane sugar, it is useful because it imparts a desirable texture to baked goods.

PURE MAPLE SYRUP. This is one sweetener that contains some health benefits, thanks to the presence of magnesium and zinc. Maple syrup, typically produced in Canada and New England, is made by tapping (that is, inserting spigots into) maple trees, collecting the sap, and boiling it down into a sweet, amber-colored syrup. Grade A syrup has a lighter color and milder flavor, while Grade B has a deeper amber color and richer maple flavor. Maple syrup is great for topping French toast, waffles, pancakes, and oatmeal, and for adding sweetness to baked goods and desserts, such as our Strawberry Rhubarb Crumb Muffins (page 64) and Maple Brown Rice Pudding (page 216).

TURBINADO SUGAR. Made from the initial pressing of sugarcane, turbinado sugar contains a bit more natural molasses in its crystals. Although there is no real nutritional value because the amount of molasses present is so small, this type of sugar will contribute more moisture to your recipe.

Nuts and Seeds

A pantry full of a wide variety of nuts and seeds is a must for any family with hungry little ones to feed. Both are rich in protein, healthy fats, and minerals, all components of a well-rounded diet. Nuts and seeds are ideal for snacking, and they add a nice crunch to salads, oatmeal, and baked goods. There are conflicting opinions and evidence as to when to introduce nuts to babies, so speak with your pediatrician about what is right for your child.

ALMONDS. Containing a high amount of good fats and proteins, almonds can easily be turned into nut butter, such as our Maple Almond Butter (page 199), as well as homemade almond milk (page 228). Also, a quick whirl in the food processor will turn almonds into almond meal, a great ingredient for gluten-free baking.

CASHEW NUTS. Cashew nuts and butter provide the body with a high dose of copper, which produces energy and helps with bone development. Cashew nuts' soft texture and mild flavor make them a favorite snack on their own, but they can easily be added to granola or whipped into cashew butter.

CHIA SEEDS. Chia seeds are one of the richest plant-based sources of omega-3 fatty acids, which enhance cognitive performance. The mild, nutty flavor of chia seeds makes them an easy addition to snacks and drinks. Sprinkle them on cereal, rice dishes, or yogurt, and mix them into smoothies and baked goods. Our Winter Granola (page 236) is a simple way to add chia seeds to your diet.

COCONUT PRODUCTS. A variety of pantry staples come from the coconut plant, including coconut milk (liquid from grated coconut meat), coconut cream (condensed coconut milk), unsweetened shredded coconut (dried grated meat), coconut water (clear liquid inside young coconuts), and coconut oil (extracted from coconut meat). Coconuts' versatile products can be used in a variety of snacks from Yogurt-Dipped Dried Fruit (page 244) to Cherry Chocolate Pudding Pops (page 50) to Grilled Nectarine Skewers with Toasted Coconut (page 142).

FLAXSEEDS. A rich source of omega-3 fatty acids, these tiny brown or golden seeds are great for adding a healthy boost to baked goods and smoothies or sprinkled over yogurt or oatmeal. We use them to give our Honey-Wheat Bread (page 202) a nutritional kick. You can find flaxseeds sold as whole seeds or ground. Both impart a slightly nutty flavor, but the whole seeds will also add a bit of a crunch, while the ground seeds won't much alter the texture of foods.

PECANS. Pecans are the most antioxidant-rich tree nut. They are a favorite addition to sweet breads, muffins, and cookies. They also make a perfect crunchy topping for creamy puddings such as our Maple Brown Rice Pudding (page 216).

PINE NUTS. An essential ingredient for both our homemade Kale Pesto and our basil pesto (pages 76 and 118), pine nuts are rich and creamy and also loaded with nutrition. A rich source of vitamins A, D, and C, they help support healthy vision, bones, and immunity.

PISTACHIO NUTS. Pistachio nuts, cracked open from their shells, will always be a simple and favorite snack on their own, but they are also great for topping our Dark-Chocolate-Dipped Coconut Macaroons (page 248). Pistachios offer fiber and protein, and their pop of green makes for festive holiday cookie decorating.

PUMPKIN SEEDS. Pumpkin seeds are a rich source of zinc, which supports a healthy immune system, growth during childhood, and wound healing. You can buy the green, hull-less seeds—also known as pepitas—to add to granola and other baked goods or to eat out of hand. Even better for snacking, you can harvest your own seeds from a fresh pumpkin; fresh seeds will have white hulls, a rich source of fiber. Try our Cinnamon and Maple Roasted Pumpkin Seeds (page 182) for a wholesome treat.

SESAME SEEDS. Whole sesame seeds are a delicate addition to dipping sauces and baked goods. Tahini, a paste made from ground sesame seeds, is the classic ingredient in hummus that gives the dip its rich creaminess. Try our Sesame Seed Candy (page 238), which calls for both raw sesame seeds and tahini.

SUNFLOWER SEEDS. Sunflower seeds, a rich source of vitamin E, give a subtle crunch to baked goods, such as our Sweet Potato–Cornmeal Muffins (page 240). When ground into a paste, they offer a nice alternative to nut butters, and sunflower seed butter can be used in sandwiches or spread onto Homemade Dried Cranberries on Sunflower Seed Butter Logs (page 190).

WALNUTS. Walnuts are a rich source of monounsaturated fats and omega-3 fatty acids, especially important for growing children and overall heart health. Use them in baked goods, such as our Cherry, Coconut, and Walnut Bread (page 80), chop them up and sprinkle over oatmeal, or even use them for a nuttier tasting pesto.

Oils

Oils are used for cooking, sautéing, making homemade salad dressing, imparting flavor, making dipping sauces, and adding heart-healthy fat to any dish. While "fat" tends to be used as a dirty word, it is a crucial part of any diet. That said, it is important to choose your fats wisely: the oils that we have recommended here all contain healthy fats, which are especially important for children, whose vital organs, including the brain, depend on fat for proper development.

BUTTERNUT SQUASH SEED OIL. An oil that can replace olive oil, butternut squash seed oil is made by roasting and pressing the seeds of butternut squashes. Great for sautéing, tossing with vegetables, making our Kale Chips with Butternut Squash Seed Oil and Sea Salt (page 162), and adding to sauces and dressings, this oil offers a rich, nutty flavor and is full of healthy monounsaturated fats and vitamin E.

EXTRA VIRGIN COCONUT OIL. Extracted from coconut flesh, this oil imparts a light coconut scent and taste when used for sautéing or in baking and smoothies. Coconut oil is a heart-healthy food that can help the body mount resistance to viruses and bacteria that can cause illness. It is also a great dry skin rub, diaper cream, cradle-cap treatment, natural lip balm, and seasoning agent for cast iron skillets.

EXTRA VIRGIN OLIVE OIL. A staple in most kitchens, olive oil is ideal for cooking, baking, dipping bread, dressing salads, seasoning cast iron, and drizzling as a finish over dips and spreads. Look for bottles labeled "extra virgin" and "first cold press" to ensure you are buying the highest-quality oil, rich in monounsaturated fatty acids. You'll find olive oil used throughout the book, but for an introduction to baking with this heart-healthy oil try our Peach Olive Oil Muffins (page 130).

TOASTED SESAME OIL. Rich, nutty, and toasty, this oil is a flavorful option for stir-fries, dressings, and Asian-inspired dishes, such as our Vegetable Dumplings (page 230). Toasted oil doesn't hold its flavor over high heat, however. Full of both monounsaturated and polyunsaturated fats, toasted sesame oil is another heart-healthy cooking option.

The Recipes

Here you'll find one hundred original, simple, easy-to-pack, whole food snack recipes grouped by season. Each chapter begins with a list of seasonal produce to guide your shopping and snacking. These fruits and vegetables are simply our favorite produce of the season; certainly include any and all of your family's favorites and unusual offerings of your region. Lists are based on a four-season year, but adjust expectations to your particular climate—for example, if you're lucky you may be already enjoying what we consider summer veggies in spring. We hope you'll experiment accordingly.

We've also given you some ideas for seasonal field trips to educate your family on where their food comes from and how it is produced. You might find a farm that allows you to pick your own fruits and vegetables or experience maple sugaring, or you might take a weekend trip to an apple orchard. Both Sarah and I live in New England, where we enjoy a four-season year. Spring brings magnolia and cherry blossoms, summer finds us at the ocean's edge every chance we get, fall ignites the mountains with fiery leaves, and winter brings mounds of snow and bottomless cups of hot chocolate. Perhaps you live in an area where the seasonal shifts are a bit less dramatic. If this is the case, your foraging adventures, like your produce options, may be a bit more varied during the winter months and more steamy during the warmer months.

As you scan the recipes, look for these symbols:

GF **GLUTEN FREE**
NF **NUT FREE**
DF **DAIRY FREE**

Also keep an eye out for two helpful call-outs:

NUTRITIONAL SUPERSTAR offers an explanation of the recipe's key health benefits, focusing on the nutritional needs of growing, active children.

BABY FRIENDLY recommends simple steps to transform the recipe into a baby-friendly (six to twelve months) option to avoid having to cook separate snacks for each member of the family.

SPRING RECIPES

Asparagus Fries with Parmesan Cheese 43
Yogurt-Granola Cups with Homemade Cherry Sauce 44
Spring Vegetable Spears with Dipping Bar 46
Honey Frozen Yogurt–Dipped Strawberries 49
Cherry Chocolate Pudding Pops 50
Strawberry Frozen Yogurt Sandwiches 52
Roasted Sesame Peas 57
Creamy Asparagus Dip with Flax Crackers 58
Raspberry French Toast Sticks 60
Ratatouille Baked Egg Cups 62
Strawberry Rhubarb Crumb Muffins 64
Leek Fritters 66
Strawberry Fruit Leather 68
Green Waffles 70
Spinach Puffs 72
Twice-Baked Mini Red Potatoes 74
Hard-Boiled Eggs with Kale Pesto 76
Cherry, Coconut, and Walnut Bread 80
Cherry Coconut Lime Flavored Ice 82
Quinoa Pudding with Raspberries and Pecans 84
Berry and Cream Scones with Whipped Honey Butter 86
Raspberry Guacamole 89
Sugar Snap Peas with Honey-Mustard Dip 90
Pea-Avocado Smoothie 93
Rhubarb-Lemon Biscotti 94

Spring

SPRING IS A TIME OF HOPE: TINY SEEDS UNFURL INTO FRAGILE SHOOTS WHILE THE WORLD, ONCE AGAIN, TURNS GREEN AND HUMS WITH NEW LIFE. THE REAPPEARANCE OF SUNNY DAYS SENDS MY BOYS RUNNING FOR THE DOOR. THEY YEARN TO BE OUTSIDE, RUNNING, jumping, and playing in the puddles. All that play means hearty appetites, and luckily spring's abundant produce promises they won't go hungry. The first spring hike begs for something sweet yet filling, like our Strawberry Rhubarb Crumb Muffins (page 64). Creamy Asparagus Dip with Flax Crackers (page 58) is a perfect snack during spring evenings spent playing at the park until the sun sets. Lazy weekend afternoons in the garden call for packable treats such as Yogurt-Granola Cups with Homemade Cherry Sauce (page 44).

Kids of all ages would probably agree that there is no greater way to experience the joy of spring than a good dig in the dirt. I am passionate about my community garden plot, which produces an astounding amount of produce in a 6-by-9-foot space: radishes, spinach, sugar snap peas, kale, lettuce, cabbage, broccoli, and more tomatoes than I know what to do with! I have been taking my boys to the garden since they were babies, letting them crawl around in the dirt and dig with toy shovels. Soil is a fascinating living ecosystem, with so many roly-poly worms and bugs for kids to explore. With every rock they overturn, and every shovelful of rich soil, my boys gain a deeper appreciation for the many layers of a healthy soil profile. As they grow and mature I give them more important jobs like planting seeds, digging up weeds, and harvesting radishes, snap peas, and cherry tomatoes.

Planting a full vegetable garden can seem overwhelming, so if you're interested in growing your own food, I suggest starting small, with a few herb pots, tomato bushes, or strawberry plants. If you have room to build a raised bed, try your hand at growing your family's favorite vegetables—maybe sugar snap peas, carrots, and radishes. Kids of all ages love dirt, so get them involved! Consider handing over the upkeep of a garden space or potted plant just to them. When kids play a role in growing food, they are often excited to eat the fruits of their labor, even if it's something they have dismissed in the past.

Spring is also an ideal time to find a CSA that meets your family's needs. Imagine what you could do with a box of farm-fresh veggies and fruits delivered weekly! The possibilities are endless, and our fruit- and vegetable-driven snack recipes will give you plenty to start with, and many ideas to jump-start your own cooking creativity.

Rhubarb and strawberries make their appearance in early spring to get things started, while late spring brings a bounty that rivals that of summer. Look for the first cherries, raspberries, and snap peas to begin appearing at the farmers' market in late spring. The first sun-ripened basket of raspberries will send juice dripping down little fingers and chins, making that long winter a distant memory.

FAVORITE SPRING PRODUCE

ARTICHOKES
ARUGULA
ASPARAGUS
BIBB LETTUCE
BROCCOLI
CAULIFLOWER
CHARD
CHERRIES
CHIVES
FENNEL
FIDDLEHEADS
GREEN BEANS
KALE
LEEKS
RADICCHIO
RADISHES
RASPBERRIES
RHUBARB
SALAD GREENS
SCALLIONS
SNOW PEA PODS
SPINACH
STRAWBERRIES
SUGAR SNAP PEAS
SUMMER SQUASH
VIDALIA ONIONS
WATERCRESS
ZUCCHINI

GF NF Asparagus Fries with Parmesan Cheese

/ MAKES 4 SNACKS /

I'm willing to bet that almost anything would taste good roasted and rolled in nutty Parmesan cheese, but fresh spring asparagus spears are especially delicious this way. The long green stems are ideal for little hands to hold and little mouths to nibble. To ensure crispiness, these treats are best eaten within a day of being made.

1 BUNCH OF ASPARAGUS
3 TABLESPOONS EXTRA VIRGIN OLIVE OIL
KOSHER SALT
¾ CUP FRESHLY GRATED PARMESAN CHEESE

1. Preheat the oven to 425°F. Trim the asparagus ends where the spears naturally snap, and toss the spears with the olive oil and a sprinkling of salt. Arrange the asparagus in a single layer on a baking sheet and roast for 20 to 30 minutes until crisp around the edges. Once the asparagus has reached a crispy brown, remove from the oven.
2. While the asparagus roasts, grate or sprinkle the Parmesan cheese onto a tray. Roll the warm spears in the cheese, gently shake off the excess, and lay the asparagus on a clean platter. Allow the cheesy spears to rest briefly so the Parmesan adheres, about 5 minutes. Gather small handfuls and place in parchment paper cones for festive serving.

High in fiber, protein, and vitamins A, C, E, and K, asparagus detoxifies the body and protects against cancer.

Chop prepared asparagus fries into tiny bite-size pieces or smash diced pieces with the back of a fork for younger babies. Asparagus can be stringy, so mash well for smaller babies.

GF NF Yogurt-Granola Cups with Homemade Cherry Sauce

/ MAKES 4 SMALL MASON JARS /

Fresh cherries are hard to resist, whether piled in a bowl for little hands to grab or cooked down into a decadent, fruity sauce. Here cherry sauce is layered with high-quality plain yogurt and a handful of granola to create an irresistible, easy-to-pack treat. Mason jars are ideal for taking this treat on the road or for storing in the fridge for a grab-and-go snack. If you plan on storing these for longer than a few hours, hold off on adding the granola to keep it crunchy until snacktime, then pile it on top. Try making these cups with our Winter Granola, page 236—we hope it becomes your favorite! To make the gluten-free and nut-free versions, use granola that omits these ingredients.

1¼ CUPS CHERRIES, PITTED
3 TABLESPOONS HONEY
⅓ CUP PLUS 2 TABLESPOONS WATER
1 TABLESPOON ARROWROOT POWDER
PINCH OF GROUND CINNAMON
⅛ TEASPOON PURE VANILLA EXTRACT
SQUEEZE OF LEMON JUICE
2 CUPS PLAIN WHOLE-MILK YOGURT
1½ CUPS OF YOUR FAVORITE GRANOLA (GLUTEN-FREE OR NUT-FREE IF YOU WISH)

1. Heat the cherries, honey, and ⅓ cup of the water in a medium saucepan over medium heat. Once the honey dissolves, turn up the heat and bring to a boil.
2. Meanwhile, in a small bowl whisk the arrowroot powder with the remaining 2 tablespoons of water until dissolved. Stir the arrowroot mixture into the cherries and let it boil for 1 minute. Turn the heat down to a low simmer and add the cinnamon and vanilla. Let the sauce simmer for a few more minutes, until it reaches the thickness of maple syrup. Remove the pan from the heat, swirl in a squirt of lemon juice, and let the mixture cool.
3. To assemble, grab 4 jars and spoon in a layer of yogurt, then some cooled cherry sauce and a layer of granola. Repeat until each jar is full.

Cherries, with their beautiful deep hue, are a rich source of cancer-fighting antioxidants.

For little ones who are already eating honey, these yogurt-granola cups are perfect; just mash any large cherry pieces before serving. If honey has not yet been introduced, simply sweeten the cherry sauce with maple syrup, or just stick to the plain yogurt, which is always a healthy option for babies who are enjoying dairy products.

GF NF DF Spring Vegetable Spears with Dipping Bar

/ MAKES 6 TO 8 SNACKS /

Sometimes when it comes to dealing with picky eaters the trick is in the presentation. While not quite a recipe, this snack idea offers kids the chance to try new vegetables in an interesting and tempting way. Providing dips that are already well loved—honey, nut or seed butter, sea salt—can encourage picky eaters to try new veggies. It doesn't hurt that spring's vegetable offerings are colorful (radishes), finger-food friendly (asparagus and snap peas), and crunchy (carrots), which makes them hard to resist and perfect for dipping.

1 BUNCH OF FRESH ASPARAGUS
1 BUNCH OF CARROTS
1 BUNCH OF RADISHES
1 CUP HONEY
1 CUP SUNFLOWER SEED BUTTER OR NUT BUTTER (SUCH AS ALMOND, CASHEW, OR PEANUT; CHOOSE SEED BUTTER FOR A NUT-FREE VERSION)
1 TABLESPOON COARSE SEA SALT

1. Wash the vegetables, then peel the carrots and cut into matchsticks, trim the bottoms off the asparagus, and slice the radishes into thin rounds. Pile the vegetables on a large tray or cutting board.
2. Arrange small dipping bowls of honey, seed or nut butter, and sea salt. Encourage snackers to experiment with different vegetable and dip combinations.

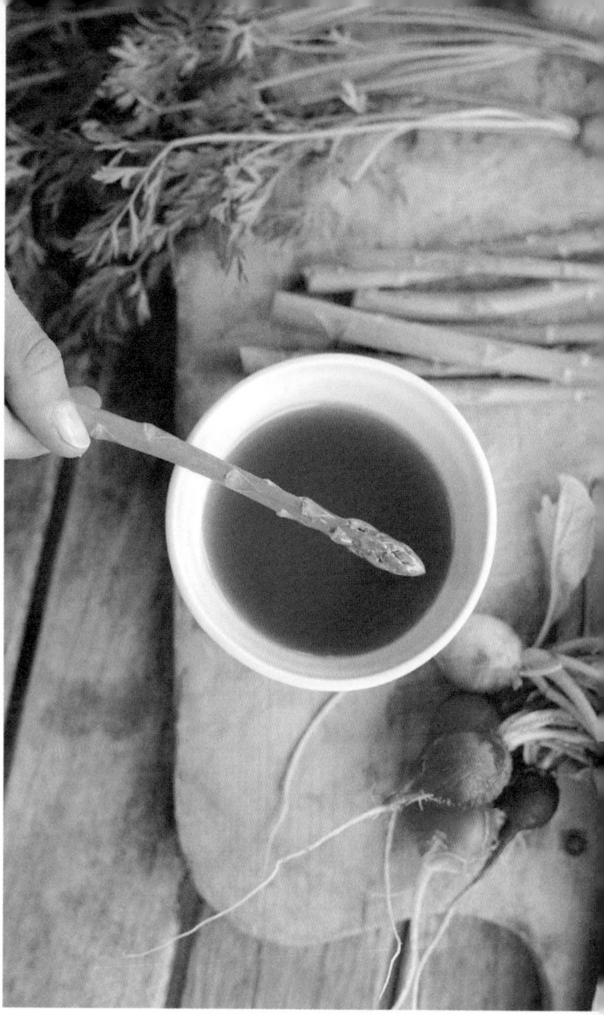

Radishes offer a healthy dose of vitamin C, which helps to rebuild tissues and blood vessels and strengthen bones and teeth.

Use a vegetable peeler to make thin ribbons from the veggies, which are easy for babies to gnaw and greatly reduces any choking risk. The dips suggested aren't well suited to babies, but you can substitute hummus, sweet potato puree, and/or our Baba Ghanoush (page 138), all of which are fun, baby-friendly dipping options.

GF NF Honey Frozen Yogurt–Dipped Strawberries

/ MAKES 2 DOZEN /

When strawberries first appear at the market I tend to go a bit wild, greedily packing my basket full. But after the boys and I gorge on the just-picked sweetness, I'm left wondering what kind of treats to make with the rest of my bounty. These simple snacks involve dipping plump berries into a sweetened mixture of yogurt and honey. After an hour in the freezer, you'll have a refreshing, slightly frozen treat that can easily be wrapped in parchment paper and thrown into a cooler with ice for an afternoon at the beach.

- 1½ CUPS PLAIN WHOLE-MILK GREEK YOGURT
- 3 TABLESPOONS HONEY
- 24 WHOLE FRESH STRAWBERRIES WITH STEMS, WASHED
- 1 WOODEN SKEWER

1. Line a baking sheet with parchment paper. In a mixing bowl combine the honey and yogurt. Stick the skewer through the stem end of a strawberry, dip and spin the strawberry in the yogurt mixture to coat, then gently lay onto the prepared baking sheet. Remove the skewer and repeat with remaining strawberries.
2. Freeze for 1 hour for the best consistency. Slice in half or eat whole.

Strawberries improve eye health and boost immunity with their powerful punch of vitamin C.

These frozen treats are perfect for older babies to hold and gnaw on, especially if new teeth are coming through. If your baby has not yet been introduced to honey, simply add a dash of vanilla extract to the yogurt instead. Smaller babies will enjoy these sliced small or thawed and smashed with a fork.

GF NF DF Cherry Chocolate Pudding Pops

/ MAKES 5 OR 6 FROZEN POPS /

Creamy, cool, and chocolaty with bright pops of cherry, these frozen treats are Sarah's answer to her son Dylan's intense love of chocolate. Instead of being loaded with sugar and heavy cream, these frozen pops rely on honey, coconut milk, and cocoa powder to bring the flavor. While ice pops may be a bit tricky to pack, with a little planning, these could make it to your next beach party: allow pops to thoroughly freeze (for a few days, if possible), keep them in their molds, and pack in a cooler full of ice for a special bring-along snack.

- ONE 13-OUNCE CAN COCONUT MILK
- ¼ CUP PLUS 1 TABLESPOON UNSWEETENED COCOA POWDER
- 2 TABLESPOONS HONEY
- 1 TEASPOON PURE VANILLA EXTRACT
- ¼ TEASPOON KOSHER SALT
- 1 CUP CHERRIES, PITTED AND ROUGHLY CHOPPED

1. Blend all the ingredients except for the cherries in a food processor until smooth. Stir the chopped cherries into the chocolate mixture and pour into ice-pop molds. Insert the sticks and freeze for at least 2 hours, until set. Loosen by quickly running the molds under warm water.

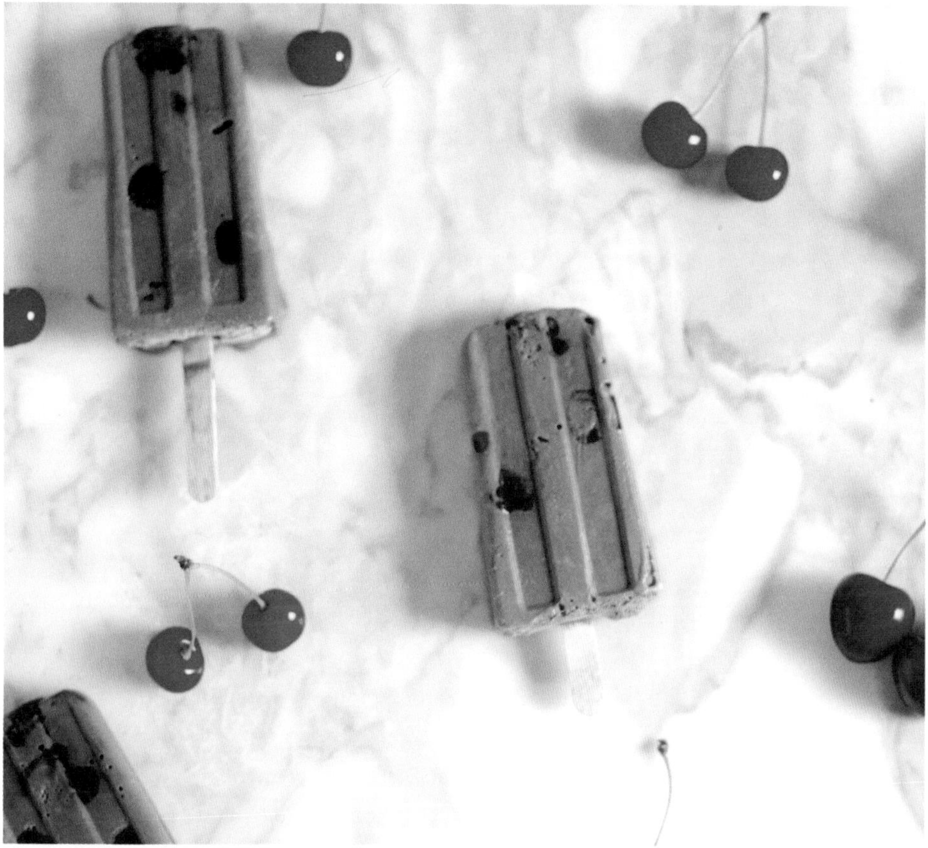

Coconut milk, a rich and creamy liquid made from the meat of mature coconuts, helps rid the body of viruses, bacteria, and countless illnesses thanks to its healthy fats, in particular lauric acid, a medium-chain saturated fatty acid.

For babies comfortable with honey and cocoa, these frozen pops are the perfect teething soother for sore gums, and the little sticks are ideal for small hands. Just be prepared for a chocolaty mess!

GF NF Strawberry Frozen Yogurt Sandwiches

/ MAKES 2 PINTS FROZEN YOGURT, FOR ABOUT 30 SANDWICHES /

Is there anything tastier than an ice cream sandwich studded with the first juicy, sun-ripened strawberries of spring? We gave things a healthy twist using Greek yogurt, along with a touch of cinnamon, vanilla, and honey for a warm, sweet flavor. While homemade cookies would be amazing, don't be afraid to take a shortcut and sandwich your homemade filling between your favorite thin, crispy grocery-store cookies (we used Anna's Thins). For the gluten-free and nut-free versions of this recipe, use cookies that omit these ingredients.

- 2 CUPS PLAIN WHOLE-MILK GREEK YOGURT
- 1½ CUPS CHOPPED FRESH STRAWBERRIES
- 1½ CUPS HEAVY WHIPPING CREAM
- ½ CUP HONEY
- 1 TABLESPOON FRESHLY SQUEEZED LEMON JUICE
- 1 TEASPOON PURE VANILLA EXTRACT
- 1 TEASPOON GROUND CINNAMON
- 60 OF YOUR FAVORITE COOKIES (GLUTEN-FREE OR NUT-FREE IF YOU WISH)

1. Whisk together all the filling ingredients in a large bowl until everything is blended and the honey is incorporated. Transfer the yogurt mixture to an ice cream maker and freeze according to the manufacturer's instructions.
2. If you don't have an ice cream maker, transfer the bowl of the yogurt mixture to the freezer. After 1 hour, take out the bowl and beat the yogurt mixture with a handheld mixer until smooth, periodically scraping down the sides of the bowl with a spatula (beating prevents the formation of ice crystals). Return the bowl to the freezer and repeat the process a few more times until the yogurt has reached an ice-cream-like consistency. This will take 5 hours or more, depending on your freezer.
3. When the yogurt is done, remove it from the freezer and allow it to soften until it becomes just scoopable. Line a baking sheet with parchment paper and place several cookies upside down on the paper. Scoop a heaping spoonful of frozen yogurt onto each cookie, then top with another cookie. Once the sand-

wiches are all made, place the baking sheet in the freezer and allow the sandwiches to harden for 20 minutes before serving. To store for later, wrap the sandwiches in parchment paper and store in the freezer.

Yogurt is full of healthy goodies including calcium, protein, and active cultures. Live cultures help to create a healthier gut environment, while the culturing process makes yogurt easier to digest than milk.

Babies who have started dairy products will greatly enjoy a few sweet spoonfuls of the strawberry frozen yogurt.

FIELD TRIP

/ VISIT A DAIRY FARM /

Finding a trusted dairy source for high-quality hormone-free cheese, cream, butter, and milk is an important step in the journey of stocking your kitchen with local foods. In some towns (such as mine, Providence, Rhode Island) there are still milkmen who deliver farm-fresh dairy products in frosted glass bottles right to the customer's door. Whether or not this option is available in your town, it's worth a trip to at least one local dairy farm to see how their operation is run and to test the quality of the goods they are producing. The best part about a spring visit is the newborn calves—a sweet sight sure to delight kids of all ages.

Many dairy farms also offer farm-fresh eggs for sale. The many labels on egg cartons can be confusing and misleading. "Organic," "Free-Range," "Vegetarian Fed"—these are mostly marketing ploys. Instead look for a local farm that offers eggs from chickens allowed access to pasture where they can forage for a natural diet of seeds, green plants, worms, and insects.

GF NF DF Roasted Sesame Peas

/ MAKES 6 TO 8 SNACKS /

Peas get a bad rap—mushy, tasteless, bland—they're often pushed around the plate and hidden under piles of mashed potatoes. But thanks to soy sauce and a pinch of ginger, this recipe gives peas a kick of flavor, and roasting them adds a hint of crunch, making for a perfectly addictive salty snack.

- 2 CUPS FRESH PEAS
- 3 TABLESPOONS EXTRA VIRGIN OLIVE OIL
- 3 TABLESPOONS LOW-SODIUM SOY SAUCE
- 1 TABLESPOON HONEY
- ¼ TEASPOON GRATED FRESH GINGER
- 2 TABLESPOONS RAW SESAME SEEDS)

1. Preheat the oven to 375°F and line a baking sheet with aluminum foil.
2. Wash and dry the peas. Whisk together the olive oil, soy sauce, honey, and ginger in a large bowl. Toss in the peas and stir until evenly coated. Spread the coated peas into a single layer on the prepared baking sheet and sprinkle with sesame seeds. Roast until crisp, about 45 minutes.

Peas supply the body with fiber, which promotes regular bowel function.

Roasted peas are a perfect finger food for babies to practice their feeding coordination. For smaller babies, crush crisp peas with a fork before serving to reduce choking risk.

Creamy Asparagus Dip with Flax Crackers

/ MAKES 2 DOZEN CRACKERS PLUS 2 CUPS OF DIP /

There is something pretty special about homemade crackers. You might wonder who has time to make such a thing, but our recipe is quick and easy with only five ingredients. Kids love rolling out the dough, so invite them to get involved. Asparagus dip flavored with toasted walnuts, herbs, and creamy ricotta cheese pairs perfectly with the crispy crunch of fresh-from-the-oven crackers. If you're looking for a gluten-free snack, swap the crackers here for your favorite gluten-free variety.

FOR THE DIP

1 BUNCH OF PENCIL-THIN GREEN ASPARAGUS, ROUGHLY CHOPPED
¼ CUP TOASTED WALNUTS
½ CUP PACKED FRESH BASIL LEAVES
¼ CUP FRESH MINT LEAVES
½ CUP WHOLE-MILK RICOTTA CHEESE
2 TABLESPOONS FRESHLY SQUEEZED LEMON JUICE
½ TEASPOON KOSHER SALT
FRESHLY GROUND BLACK PEPPER
½ CUP EXTRA VIRGIN OLIVE OIL

FOR THE CRACKERS

1½ CUPS UNBLEACHED ALL-PURPOSE FLOUR, PLUS MORE

1. To make the dip, pulse the asparagus and walnuts in a food processor until finely chopped. Add the basil, mint, ricotta, lemon juice, salt, and a few grinds of pepper. Turn on the machine and stream in the olive oil. Continue processing until smooth. Taste, and adjust the salt and pepper as needed. Refrigerate until ready to eat.
2. Position the rack in the lower third of the oven and heat to 450°F.
3. To make the crackers, whisk together the flours and 1 teaspoon of the salt in a large bowl. Add the olive oil and ½ cup water to the flour mixture, then stir with a spatula until it collects into a ball of dough. Use your hands to press the dough against the sides of the bowl to gather all the crumbs. Divide the dough into 2 balls. Transfer one dough ball onto a lightly floured surface and pat it into a rough cube. With a rolling pin, roll the dough into a 4 × 12-inch rectangle. If things start to get sticky, lift an edge of the dough and dust underneath with more flour. Brush the dough lightly with water and sprinkle evenly with 1 tablespoon of the

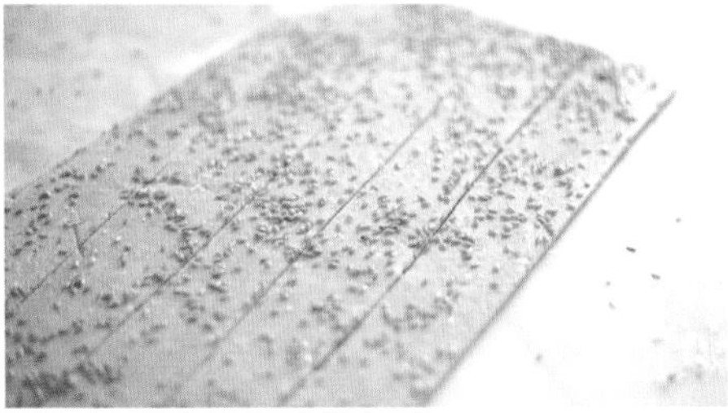

FOR ROLLING

½ CUP WHOLE WHEAT FLOUR

1½ TEASPOONS KOSHER SALT

3 TABLESPOONS EXTRA VIRGIN OLIVE OIL

½ CUP WATER

2 TABLESPOONS FLAXSEEDS, DIVIDED

flaxseeds and ¼ teaspoon of the salt. With a pizza cutter or sharp knife, cut the dough in half lengthwise, then in half again, and cut each half across into thirds to make rectangles roughly 2 by 4 inches. Repeat this with the second dough ball. Don't worry about creating perfect pieces. Carefully transfer the rectangles to a baking sheet and bake until nicely browned, about 10 minutes. Let the crackers cool on a wire rack. They can be stored for up to a week in an airtight container.

Flaxseeds contain a wealth of omega-3 fatty acids, good fats that promote heart health and aid in cancer prevention.

The creamy texture of this dip is perfect for baby. Older babies will enjoy it on the crisp crackers, but younger babies may want a softer base of bread.

GF NF Raspberry French Toast Sticks

/ MAKES 18 TOAST STICKS /

French toast is a favorite breakfast dish in our home. When I found myself packing leftovers to bring to the playground, I knew I was onto something good. While French toast might not seem like the most portable snack, cutting the slices into sticks and packing a dipping sauce in a separate container makes it a convenient on-the-go treat. The quick and easy raspberry sauce is much less sticky than maple syrup—and healthier to boot! Substitute your favorite light loaf of gluten-free bread for a gluten-free snack.

FOR THE RASPBERRY SAUCE

1½ CUPS FRESH RASPBERRIES

1 TABLESPOON HONEY

1 TABLESPOON WATER

FOR THE FRENCH TOAST STICKS

4 EGGS

1½ CUPS HEAVY CREAM, HALF-AND-HALF, OR WHOLE MILK

2 TABLESPOONS PURE VANILLA EXTRACT

½ TEASPOON GROUND CINNAMON

PINCH OF KOSHER SALT

6 BREAD SLICES (1 INCH THICK),

1. For the raspberry sauce, process the raspberries, honey, and water in a food processor until they form a smooth puree. Pour it into a fine mesh strainer over a glass container, then, using a spatula, press the puree through the strainer to create a smooth sauce. Discard the seeds left in the strainer and set aside the container of sauce.
2. To make the French toast sticks, whisk together the eggs, cream, vanilla, cinnamon, and salt in a medium bowl. Arrange the bread slices in a shallow baking dish large enough to hold all six slices in a single layer. Pour the egg mixture over the bread and let soak for 10 minutes. Turn the slices over and continue to soak for another 10 minutes.

PREFERABLY DAY-OLD CHALLAH OR BRIOCHE (OR GLUTEN-FREE BREAD IF YOU WISH)

½ STICK (4 TABLESPOONS) UNSALTED BUTTER

3. Heat 2 tablespoons of the butter in a large skillet over medium heat. Working in batches, fry the bread slices until golden brown, 2 to 3 minutes per side. Between batches, wipe down the skillet and freshen with butter. Slice each piece of French toast into thirds and serve with the raspberry sauce for dipping.

Raspberries are nutritional powerhouses packed with vitamin C, which promotes a healthy immune system.

Babies of all ages will love the sweetness of these French toast sticks. Older babies can simply grab a stick and practice dipping, while younger babies will enjoy bite-size pieces. If your baby has not yet been introduced to honey, simply omit it.

GF NF Ratatouille Baked Egg Cups

/ MAKES 12 STANDARD MUFFINS OR 20 MINI MUFFINS /

The perfect mix of vegetables and protein, this powerhouse snack is hearty, filling, and easy to pack. Try making these in mini-muffin tins, which yield bite-size frittata-like snacks. While they are delicious right out of the oven all warm and cheesy, they also store well in a lidded glass container or wrapped in parchment paper or aluminum foil.

½ RED BELL PEPPER
½ TOMATO
½ ZUCCHINI
½ SMALL SUMMER SQUASH
2 TABLESPOONS EXTRA VIRGIN OLIVE OIL
9 EGGS
½ CUP HEAVY CREAM
½ TEASPOON KOSHER SALT

1. Preheat the oven to 350°F. Line a 12-cup muffin tin with paper liners or grease a 24-cup mini-muffin tin.
2. Chop the bell pepper, tomato, zucchini, and summer squash into ¼-inch dice. Heat the olive oil in a skillet over medium heat and sauté the vegetables until soft, about 10 minutes. Remove the skillet from the heat and let cool.
3. In a large bowl whisk the eggs, cream, and salt. Divide the vegetable mixture evenly among the muffin cups, then carefully fill each cup to three-quarters full with the egg mixture. Bake standard-size cups for 15 to 20 minutes and bake mini cups for slightly less time, until the egg is puffed and just set in the center. Egg cups will keep in an airtight container in the refrigerator for 2 days. They are best enjoyed warm or at room temperature and can be easily reheated in a low oven or toaster oven.

Zucchini is packed with vitamin A, which promotes healthy liver function, eyesight, and skin.

The soft texture and small bites of vegetables in these egg cups make it a perfect snack for baby.

Strawberry Rhubarb Crumb Muffins

/ MAKES 12 MUFFINS /

Crumb topping is Sarah's secret dessert weapon. In fact, her son Dylan often gobbles the topping right off peach pies and blueberry crumbles before diving into the filling. These muffins boast a salty, crunchy crumb topping loaded with cinnamon and walnuts, which elevates this baked good from ordinary to pure decadence. No doubt the topping will be the first thing to go! Strawberry and rhubarb, the most perfect spring pairing, come together to form the base of this moist, delectable muffin sweetened with maple syrup and dark brown sugar.

FOR THE CRUMB TOPPING

- 1/3 CUP UNBLEACHED ALL-PURPOSE FLOUR
- ¼ CUP WHOLE WHEAT FLOUR
- 2 TABLESPOONS PACKED DARK BROWN SUGAR
- ¼ TEASPOON GROUND CINNAMON
- PINCH OF SEA SALT
- 3 TABLESPOONS CHOPPED WALNUTS
- 3 TABLESPOONS COLD UNSALTED BUTTER, CUT INTO SMALL CUBES
- 2 TABLESPOONS PURE MAPLE SYRUP

1. Preheat the oven to 400°F degrees and line a 12-cup muffin tin with paper liners.
2. To make the crumb topping, combine the flours, sugar, cinnamon, salt, and walnuts in a small bowl. Cut in the butter with your fingers until small pebbles of dough form, then stir in the maple syrup.
3. To make the muffins, pour the slightly cooled melted butter into a bowl. Stir in the egg, sugar, maple syrup, yogurt, and vanilla. In a separate bowl, stir together the flours, baking powder, baking soda, salt, and ginger. Add the wet mixture to the dry mixture and stir until just combined. The batter will be thick. Gently fold in the rhubarb and strawberries.
4. With an ice cream scoop or large spoon evenly distribute the batter among the prepared muffin cups and top with crumble, pressing it gently into batter. Bake for 20 to 25 minutes, until a toothpick inserted into the center of a muffin comes out clean. Let the muffins cool for at least 15 minutes before digging in.

FOR THE MUFFIN BATTER

1 STICK (½ CUP) UNSALTED BUTTER, MELTED

1 EGG

¼ CUP PACKED DARK BROWN SUGAR

¼ CUP PURE MAPLE SYRUP

¾ CUP PLAIN WHOLE-MILK GREEK YOGURT

1 TEASPOON PURE VANILLA EXTRACT

1 CUP WHOLE WHEAT FLOUR

½ CUP UNBLEACHED ALL-PURPOSE FLOUR

1½ TEASPOONS BAKING POWDER

¼ TEASPOON BAKING SODA

¼ TEASPOON KOSHER SALT

½ TEASPOON GROUND GINGER

¾ CUP DICED FRESH RHUBARB, ABOUT 2 STALKS

1 HEAPING CUP CHOPPED FRESH STRAWBERRIES

Muffins sealed in an airtight container will keep for up to 3 days. To reheat, warm the muffins in a low oven or slice in half and toast slightly for best results.

Rhubarb offers powerful antioxidants for general immune system support.

Babies who have enjoyed walnuts can dig right in to these fruity muffins. If your little one has yet to experiment with nuts, simply leave the topping off a few of the filled muffin cups before baking and break up the muffins into finger food.

Leek Fritters

/ MAKES 8 TO 10 FRITTERS /

Leeks might seem a bit highbrow for little palates, but their versatility makes them a staple in our kitchens. Leeks look like overgrown green onions, and their flavor is similar to that of an onion but without the intensity. They are much more mild, almost buttery, when cooked down, as they are in this recipe. Because the bottoms of the leeks grow below ground and are made up of intricate layers, thorough washing is essential, and it's a great task for kids. Fill up a large pot of cold water and let your children slosh around the chopped leeks to remove all residue. Lemony yogurt sauce, with its citrus-forward flavors, perfectly complements these crispy, savory fritters. Pack the yogurt sauce in a mason jar and wrap the fritters in aluminum foil for easy travels, or eat them straight out of the skillet for a warm, satisfying snack.

FOR THE SAUCE

½ CUP PLAIN WHOLE-MILK GREEK YOGURT
½ CUP SOUR CREAM
1 GARLIC CLOVE
2 TABLESPOONS FRESHLY SQUEEZED LEMON JUICE
2 TABLESPOONS EXTRA VIRGIN OLIVE OIL
½ TEASPOON KOSHER SALT

1. To make the sauce, simply process all the ingredients in a food processor, then transfer to a small bowl and set aside.
2. To make the fritters, cut the white and pale green parts of the leeks into 1-inch slices, then rinse well (dirt likes to hide between the layers) and dry on a kitchen towel. You should have about 3 cups. Discard the dark green tops. In a skillet over medium heat, sauté the leeks and onion in ¼ cup of the olive oil for about 10 minutes, stirring every few minutes, until soft. Transfer the mixture to a large bowl and add the parsley, cumin, cinnamon, sugar, and salt. Allow the mixture to cool.
3. In a separate bowl, stir together the flour, baking powder, egg, milk, and butter to form a batter. Add the batter to the cooled vegetable mixture and stir gently to combine.
4. Line a baking sheet with paper towels.

FOR THE FRITTERS

3 LEEKS

¾ CUP FINELY CHOPPED YELLOW ONION

½ CUP EXTRA VIRGIN OLIVE OIL

½ CUP FINELY CHOPPED FRESH PARSLEY

1 TEASPOON GROUND CUMIN

¼ TEASPOON GROUND CINNAMON

1 TEASPOON PURE CANE SUGAR

½ TEASPOON KOSHER SALT

¾ CUP UNBLEACHED ALL-PURPOSE FLOUR

2 TABLESPOONS BAKING POWDER

1 EGG

⅔ CUP MILK

½ STICK (4 TABLESPOONS) UNSALTED BUTTER, MELTED

5 Heat a large skillet over medium-high heat and add 2 tablespoons of the olive oil. Using a ¼ cup measure, spoon a few large dollops of batter onto the skillet, flatten into a fritter, and fry for 2 to 3 minutes on each side, until nicely browned. Transfer to the paper towels to absorb excess oil and let them cool. Continue cooking up fritters, adding 2 more tablespoons of oil as needed. Serve warm or at room temperature with dipping sauce on the side or drizzled on top. To store fritters, layer them between sheets of parchment paper and place in an airtight glass container. They will keep in the refrigerator for up to 4 days. To freeze, wrap fritters individually or layer with parchment paper in a container.

Leeks supply the body with vitamin A, which supports nose, throat, urinary-tract, and digestive-tract health.

Older babies will be happy to feed themselves a whole leek fritter, while younger babies will enjoy bite-size pieces. Sauce can be spread or drizzled over the top, but if you are up for a bit of a mess, allow dipping!

GF NF DF Strawberry Fruit Leather

/ MAKES 6 TO 8 ROLLS /

I distinctly remember lusting after the overly sweet, bright red ropes of fruit leather that all my grade school friends were "lucky" enough to have packed in their lunch boxes. Looking at the ingredient list as an adult, I now feel like the lucky one for having been spared the food coloring and preservatives. As proved by this recipe, there is no need to mess with what nature provides. Strawberries, a twist of lemon, agave, and a bit of patience are all that's needed for a wholesome re-creation of this childhood favorite.

1 TABLESPOON CANOLA OIL
2 POUNDS FRESH STRAWBERRIES, STEMS AND HULLS REMOVED, SLICED IN HALF
JUICE OF 1 LEMON
½ CUP WATER
2 TABLESPOONS AGAVE NECTAR

1. Preheat the oven to 200°F. Line a small baking sheet or 9 × 11-inch baking pan with parchment paper, then brush paper with the canola oil.
2. Put the strawberries, lemon juice, and water into a large saucepot over medium high heat. Simmer the fruit mixture for 15 minutes, or until the strawberries are soft and smell delicious. Carefully pour the mixture into a blender and add the agave nectar. Blend until smooth.
3. Pour the strawberry puree onto the prepared baking sheet and bake in the warm oven for up to 5 hours. The fruit leather is ready when the top is still slightly sticky but it comes easily off the parchment paper when tugged. Remove the fruit leather from the baking sheet, peeling it off the paper as you go, and slice it into long strips with a pizza cutter or sharp knife. Stored in a lidded glass container or wrapped in beeswax wrap, fruit leather will stay fresh in the refrigerator for up to 5 days.

Strawberries' anti-inflammatory properties may help to alleviate symptoms of allergies including runny nose, watery eyes, and hives.

Strawberry fruit leather is an ideal snack for babies to hold and suck on—just keep the pieces small.

NF Green Waffles

/ MAKES 8 TO 10 SNACKS /

Green waffles? Sounds like they belong in a Dr. Seuss rhyme. But these savory waffles are so flavorful and full of good greens that kids won't think twice about the color. Flecks of spinach, cilantro, and scallions combine for a flavorful, savory blend. Make enough to freeze; they can be reheated easily in the oven or toaster for a satisfying snack.

- 8 OUNCES (ABOUT 8 CUPS) SPINACH, WASHED
- 2 TABLESPOONS CHOPPED FRESH CILANTRO
- 6 SCALLIONS, SLICED THIN
- 2 CUPS UNBLEACHED ALL-PURPOSE FLOUR
- 2 TEASPOONS BAKING POWDER
- 1 TEASPOON BAKING SODA
- ½ TEASPOON KOSHER SALT
- GRATED ZEST OF 1 LIME
- 1 TEASPOON GROUND CUMIN
- 2 CUPS LOW-FAT BUTTERMILK
- 1 STICK (½ CUP) UNSALTED BUTTER, MELTED
- 2 EGGS
- VEGETABLE OIL, FOR GREASING THE WAFFLE IRON

1. Preheat the waffle iron.
2. Wilt the spinach in a skillet with a splash of water. Let the spinach cool, squeeze out all the liquid, and chop fine. Put the spinach into a small bowl and stir in the cilantro and scallions.
3. In a medium bowl, whisk together the flour, baking powder, baking soda, salt, lime zest, and cumin. In a separate bowl, whisk together the buttermilk, butter, and eggs. Add the flour mixture to the wet ingredients and gently stir to combine. Add the spinach mixture and stir to combine.
4. Brush the hot waffle iron with vegetable oil and pour enough batter onto the iron to leave a ½-inch border on all sides, spreading the batter if necessary (the amount will depend on the size of your waffle iron). Close the iron and cook until the waffles are golden brown and crisp, 3 to 5 minutes. Repeat with the remaining batter. Eat immediately and freeze any leftovers for easy toasting.

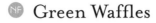

Scallions provide a high dose of vitamin K, which keeps bones healthy.

Smaller babies can enjoy bite-size waffle pieces, while older babies can hold and munch a whole waffle.

NF Spinach Puffs

/ MAKES 8 PUFFS /

Inspired by spanakopita, the popular savory Greek pastry otherwise known as spinach pie, these tender puffs pack a punch of daily greens thanks to a hearty dose of flavorful spinach tucked into layers of crispy phyllo dough. Goat cheese adds a creamy tang to the filling, while garlic and onion brighten the flavor of the spinach. Puffs are best eaten warm from the oven, but they hold up well wrapped in aluminum foil or stored in a lidded glass container.

- 8 OUNCES (ABOUT 8 CUPS) SPINACH, WASHED
- ½ CUP CRUMBLED GOAT CHEESE
- ¼ CUP GRATED ONION
- 1 TABLESPOON EXTRA VIRGIN OLIVE OIL
- 2 GARLIC CLOVES, MINCED
- KOSHER SALT AND GROUND BLACK PEPPER
- 1 EGG
- 1 TABLESPOON UNSALTED BUTTER, MELTED
- 4 SHEETS FROZEN PHYLLO DOUGH, THAWED AND KEPT CHILLED

1. Preheat the oven to 400°F.
2. Wilt the spinach in a large skillet with a splash of water. Let the spinach cool, squeeze out all the liquid, and chop fine. In a medium bowl, stir together the chopped spinach, goat cheese, onion, olive oil, garlic, and salt and pepper to taste. Beat the egg in a small bowl and fold into the spinach mixture.
3. Lay 1 sheet of phyllo dough on a clean work surface and brush with melted butter. Layer on the second sheet, brush with butter again, lay on third sheet, brush with butter, and finally top with the fourth layer. Cut the layered phyllo dough in half lengthwise, in half crosswise, then into 8 equal rectangles. Place the squares into cups of a muffin tin, pressing them into the bottom and against the sides and leaving the corners pointing up.
4. Distribute the spinach filling among the pastry-lined cups. Bake until the puffs are golden brown, about 7 to 10 minutes. Enjoy warm from the oven. Store spinach puffs in an airtight container in the refrigerator for up to 4 days.

Spinach has a long list of health benefits including an abundance of vitamin K, which contributes to a healthy nervous system.

Spinach puffs' round shape and soft texture make them an ideal snack for babies. Younger babies will enjoy small pieces of the pastry and spinach filling.

GF NF Twice-Baked Mini Red Potatoes

/ MAKES 12 STUFFED POTATOES /

Baby red potatoes are the perfect bite-size treat, especially when filled with creamy, cheesy goodness and flecked with thyme. The last time I made these my boys ate them straight out of the oven, practically burning their mouths as they shoveled them in. I had a hard time convincing them to save a single one for snack time, but if you can hold on to a few, they can be easily packed either wrapped in aluminum foil or stored in a lidded glass container. Although tastiest when served warm, they are quite good at room temperature too.

- 12 BABY RED POTATOES, EACH ABOUT 1 INCH IN DIAMETER
- 1 TABLESPOON EXTRA VIRGIN OLIVE OIL
- 1 TEASPOON CHOPPED FRESH THYME
- 1 TEASPOON KOSHER SALT, PLUS MORE FOR SPRINKLING
- ½ TEASPOON GROUND BLACK PEPPER
- ¼ CUP SOUR CREAM
- ¼ CUP COARSELY GRATED PARMESAN CHEESE

1. Preheat the oven to 425°F.
2. Toss the potatoes and the olive oil on a baking sheet. Sprinkle with ½ teaspoon of the thyme, ½ teaspoon of the salt, ¼ teaspoon of the pepper, and toss again. Bake the seasoned potatoes until they are easily pierced with a skewer, 20 to 25 minutes. Remove the baking sheet from the oven and let the potatoes rest until cool enough to handle, about 10 minutes. Increase the oven temperature to 450°F.
3. Carefully slice off the top of each potato. Score the exposed flesh with a knife and use a small spoon or a melon baller to scoop out most of the center flesh into a large bowl. Save the potato tops for another dish (such as home fries or potato salad).
4. Mash the potato flesh with a fork, then add the sour cream and the remaining ½ teaspoon of thyme, ½ teaspoon of salt, and ¼ teaspoon of pepper. Using a small spoon and your fingers, fill the hollow potatoes with the mixture, overstuffing each a bit. Sprinkle the Parmesan cheese on top.

5. Return the potatoes to the oven and bake until the filling heats through and the tops are crisp, 8 to 10 minutes. Sprinkle the potatoes with salt immediately after taking them out of the oven (they benefit from the extra seasoning).

Red potatoes offer iron, potassium, and vitamin C along with vitamin B6, which plays numerous roles in our nervous system, many of which involve brain-cell activity.

Smash a stuffed potato with the back of a fork to form a flat pancake for a snack for an older baby. For a younger baby, set aside some of the potato flesh before adding seasonings.

GF Hard-Boiled Eggs with Kale Pesto

/ MAKES 6 SNACKS /

I'm lucky enough to be raising backyard chickens, which means fresh eggs abound at our home. Hard-boiled eggs are a favorite snack, packed full of good fats and loads of protein. Kale pesto as a dipping sauce gives this standby snack a healthy boost of greens. Our pesto has heart-healthy garlic, toasty pine nuts, and freshly grated Pecorino cheese to thank for its strong flavors. Pesto is best at room temperature, though hard-boiled eggs should be kept chilled until served.

6 EGGS

FOR THE PESTO

2 CUPS PACKED FRESH BASIL LEAVES
4 KALE LEAVES, STEMS REMOVED
2 GARLIC CLOVES
¼ CUP PINE NUTS, TOASTED
½ CUP EXTRA VIRGIN OLIVE OIL
⅓ CUP FRESHLY GRATED PECORINO CHEESE
KOSHER SALT AND GROUND BLACK PEPPER

1. Put the eggs into a saucepan and fill with water until the eggs are covered by one inch. Bring the water to a boil, then cover and remove from the heat. Let the eggs and hot water stand for 8 minutes, then drain and let the eggs cool.
2. To make the pesto, put the basil, kale, garlic, and pine nuts into a food processor and pulse until coarsely chopped. Turn on the processor and stream in the olive oil. Process until the pesto is smooth, then pour into a bowl and stir in the cheese. Add salt and pepper to taste.
3. To serve, slice cooled eggs in half and serve with a small cup of kale pesto for dipping.

Kale contains more iron than beef. Adequate iron helps transport oxygen to various parts of the body, aids cell growth, and encourages proper liver function.

Egg yolk is a perfect first food for babies, as it is packed with protein, fat, vitamins, and minerals. For babies as young as six months, mix a hard-boiled egg yolk with a bit of water to thin it out. A crumbled whole hard-boiled egg is a fast and simple food for older babies. For babies who enjoy nuts, toss egg bits in a small amount of pesto to lightly coat.

FIELD TRIP

/ SPRING AT THE NURSERY /

Spring is the perfect time to visit a plant nursery with your kids and pick out a few fun herb or vegetable seedlings to grow together as a family. If you already have a vegetable garden, then an annual trip (or three!) to the nursery is nothing new. But for beginner gardeners, spring is the perfect time to stock up on seedlings of easy-to-grow vegetables such as basil, mint, kale, and lettuces. The nursery staff can guide you to the right plants to fit your requirements—drought resistance or shade tolerance, for example. For a simple first gardening project, plant a few small pots of herbs and let older children take responsibility for the watering and for harvesting at mealtime. You don't even need an outdoor space—a sunny windowsill will do just fine.

I also love picking up a few packets of wildflower seeds while at the nursery. We had a sunny, barren patch of dirt next to our driveway, and with the boys help I turned the soil, added some compost, and scattered seeds. We were rewarded with a bright, wild, untamed patch of colorful wildflowers right in our backyard. The boys loved helping me cut bouquets with their child-size gardening sheers.

Cherry, Coconut, and Walnut Bread

/ MAKES 1 LOAF /

This versatile bread packed with nutty coconut, toasted walnuts, and sweet cherries can take you from breakfast straight through to dessert. Individual slices wrapped in parchment paper are ideal for an on-the-go breakfast or tucked into a lunch box. For an extra-decadent dessert, add dark chocolate chunks and serve the slices straight from the oven topped with a dollop of vanilla frozen yogurt. There won't be a crumb left!

- ⅓ CUP UNSALTED BUTTER, MELTED
- ¾ CUP LIGHT BROWN SUGAR
- 1 EGG, BEATEN
- 1 TEASPOON PURE VANILLA EXTRACT
- 1 TEASPOON GROUND CINNAMON
- 1¼ CUP UNBLEACHED ALL-PURPOSE FLOUR
- 1 TEASPOON BAKING SODA
- PINCH OF KOSHER SALT
- 1 CUP CHERRIES, PITTED AND ROUGHLY CHOPPED
- ¼ CUP UNSWEETENED SHREDDED COCONUT
- ½ CUP RAW WALNUTS, TOASTED AND CHOPPED

1. Preheat the oven to 350°F and grease a 4 × 8-inch loaf pan.
2. In a large bowl, whisk together the butter, sugar, egg, vanilla, and cinnamon. In a separate small bowl, whisk together the flour, baking soda, and salt. Add the dry mixture to the wet mixture and stir until just combined. Gently fold in the cherries, coconut, and walnuts.
3. Pour the mixture into the loaf pan. Bake for 50 to 60 minutes, until a toothpick inserted into the center comes out clean. Place the pan on a wire rack and let it cool. Remove the bread from the pan and slice if serving immediately. Uncut Cherry, Coconut, and Walnut Bread will keep on the countertop for 3 days wrapped in parchment paper or beeswax wrap. Bread slices are best enjoyed slightly toasted after the day of baking.

The antioxidant and anti-inflammatory benefits of walnuts are well documented. Additionally, walnuts are a rich source of monounsaturated fats and omega-3 fatty acids, especially important nutrients for growing children.

This soft and sweet bread is perfect for babies who enjoy nuts. If your baby doesn't eat nuts, we recommend dividing the dough between two bowls before adding the walnuts and then adding ¼ cup nuts to only one of the bowls. Bake in two mini-loaf pans.

GF NF DF Cherry Coconut Lime Flavored Ice

/ MAKES 8 POPS /

The most popular parents of my grade school softball teammates were those who brought flavored ice for the after-game snack. We'd swarm the cooler vying for the best flavors, waiting patiently for the plastic tops to be snipped before slurping up the icy goodness. Come to find out, the beloved flavored ices of my youth are primarily made of sugar, dyes, artificial flavorings, and water. Our recipe eliminates the fake stuff, and instead ripe cherries, coconut milk, and a twist of lime bring the fruity flavor. There are endless combinations to experiment with: blackberry peach, honeydew lime, raspberry lemon, mango mint, and the list goes on. This is one place where plastic is hard to beat. I recommend Zipzicles, which are specifically for making flavored ice.

2 CUP FROZEN OR FRESH CHERRIES, PITTED
1¼ CUP COCONUT MILK (BOUGHT IN THE NUT MILK SECTION, NOT FROM A CAN)
¼ CUP FRESHLY SQUEEZED LIME JUICE (FROM 1 TO 2 LIMES)
2 TABLESPOONS HONEY

1. Blend the cherries, coconut milk, lime, and honey in a blender until smooth. Using a funnel or turkey baster, fill the individual flavored-ice pouches. Allow to freeze for 2 hours before enjoying.

Cherries are a rich source of antioxidants, including melatonin, which helps regulate the body's natural sleep patterns. A handful of cherries or a glass of cherry juice after dinner can make for a more restful night's sleep.

Teething babies will be soothed by these fruity treats; just watch out for larger bites that may be hard for babies to handle. If younger infants have trouble holding on to the cold tubes, you can squeeze out the snack into a bowl and allow it to thaw slightly to a slushy consistency for spoon feeding.

GF NF Quinoa Pudding with Raspberries and Pecans

/ MAKES 6 SNACKS /

A healthier take on traditional white rice pudding, our quinoa pudding has a rich, warm flavor thanks to hints of vanilla and cinnamon. Sarah's boys love this sweet treat topped with farm-fresh raspberries and crunchy toasted pecans. The toppings add flavor and texture to the otherwise creamy concoction. Have fun experimenting with different fruits, nuts, and seeds to find your favorite combination of toppings.

- 1 CUP UNCOOKED QUINOA
- 3 CUPS WHOLE MILK
- 1 CUP HEAVY CREAM
- ¼ CUP AGAVE NECTAR
- PINCH OF KOSHER SALT
- 1 TEASPOON PURE VANILLA EXTRACT
- ½ TEASPOON GROUND CINNAMON
- 1 CUP FRESH RASPBERRIES
- 1 CUP RAW PECANS, TOASTED AND CHOPPED (OPTIONAL; OMIT FOR NUT-FREE VERSION)
- PURE MAPLE SYRUP, FOR SERVING

1. Put the quinoa into a strainer and rinse under cold water for a few seconds and set aside. Stir together the milk, cream, agave, salt, vanilla, and cinnamon in a medium saucepan and bring to a low boil. Add the quinoa and stir. Reduce the heat to medium-low, keeping the pudding at a strong simmer. Place a lid on the pot a little askew. Cook for about 30 minutes, stirring every few minutes, until the quinoa is tender. If a skin starts to form on top of the milk, just stir it to break it up.
2. While the pudding cooks, put the raspberries into a small bowl and mash with the back of a fork until juicy. When the pudding is ready to eat, ladle it into bowls or jars and top with mashed raspberries, a sprinkling of pecans, and a drizzle of maple syrup. The pudding is best eaten warm or at room temperature. Leftovers can be stored in the refrigerator for up to 5 days and reheated slowly in a saucepan over low heat. Add a splash of milk to loosen up the cold grains when reheating.

Quinoa's most striking health benefit is its overall nutrient richness. The small grain is packed with goodness—from protein to healthy fats to vitamin E and calcium—supporting everything from bone health to cancer prevention.

Quinoa pudding is an ideal nutrient-rich snack for baby. Depending on your baby's tastes, swirl in mashed raspberries or drizzle with maple syrup for extra sweetness.

NF Berry and Cream Scones with Whipped Honey Butter

/ MAKES 8 SCONES /

Few bakeries seem to get the scone right; I often find them dry, tasteless, and a bit too crumbly for my taste. Sarah and I knew there was a more appealing approach, one that would render a light, fluffy scone loaded with flavor. Studded with sweet berries and the zest of an orange, our scones are big on flavor, and thanks to a healthy dollop of cream, they are as light as air. When paired with whipped honey butter, I can promise they will become a snack time (and, of course, breakfast) favorite. Dare I say your search for the perfect scone ends here?

FOR THE SCONES

2 CUPS UNBLEACHED ALL-PURPOSE FLOUR
1 TABLESPOON BAKING POWDER
1 TEASPOON KOSHER SALT
7 TABLESPOONS COLD UNSALTED BUTTER, CUT INTO SMALL CUBES
1½ CUPS FRESH BERRIES (BLUEBERRIES, RASPBERRIES, BLACKBERRIES, STRAWBERRIES, OR A MIX)
3 TABLESPOONS AGAVE NECTAR
GRATED ZEST OF 1 ORANGE
⅓ CUP PLUS 2 TABLESPOONS HEAVY CREAM
2 EGGS

1. Position the rack in the middle of the oven and preheat to 400°F.
2. To make the scones, put the flour, baking powder, and salt into the bowl of a food processor and pulse to combine. Sprinkle the cubes of butter evenly over the flour mixture and pulse a dozen times. Transfer the flour mixture to a large bowl.
3. In a small bowl, whisk together the agave nectar, orange zest, ⅓ cup of the cream, and the eggs. Add the cream mixture to the flour mixture and gently fold in, folding in the berries at the same time. The dough should be sticky.
4. Transfer the dough onto a well-floured surface and pat into a ball with floured hands. To form scones, press the ball into a thick round disk, then cut the dough into 8 wedges. Arrange the wedges on an ungreased baking sheet, brush with the remaining 2 tablespoons of cream, and sprinkle with sugar. Bake until the tops are light brown, about 20 minutes. Transfer the scones to a wire rack and let cool for at least 10 minutes.

1 TABLESPOON TURBINADO OR OTHER COARSE RAW SUGAR

FOR THE HONEY BUTTER

2 STICKS (1 CUP) UNSALTED BUTTER, AT ROOM TEMPERATURE

¼ CUP HONEY

½ TEASPOON GROUND CINNAMON

½ TEASPOON PURE VANILLA EXTRACT

5. To make the honey butter, put the butter, honey, cinnamon, and vanilla into a medium bowl and beat with an electric mixer for 5 minutes. Leftover butter can be spooned onto parchment paper, rolled into a log, and refrigerated.
6. Serve scones warm or at room temperature with the butter. Scones keep best wrapped in parchment paper or beeswax wrap or stored in a lidded glass container on the countertop for up to 3 days.

Blueberries' vast array of antioxidant nutrients improve cognitive function and eye health and support the cardiovascular system.

Berry and Cream Scones are an easy food for baby to enjoy. Older babies can hold a full scone, while smaller babies will enjoy bite-size pieces.

GF NF DF Raspberry Guacamole

/ MAKES ABOUT 2 CUPS /

Guacamole with raspberries? It sounds a bit crazy, but you'll just have to trust us. Avocado was a first food for Sarah's babies, and when they reached toddlerhood, she tossed small cubes of avocado and mango together for a sweet blend. The inspiration for this unique pairing came from the idea of mixing sweet with savory, turning classic guacamole on its head. We found the tanginess of raspberries to be even more delicious with avocado than the mango. With either fruit, the added pop of sweetness lends a wonderful note to the otherwise creamy, savory mixture.

3 RIPE AVOCADOS
1 TEASPOON KOSHER SALT
JUICE OF 1 LIME
¼ CUP FINELY CHOPPED FRESH CILANTRO
¼ CUP GRATED ONION
½ CUP RASPBERRIES
TORTILLA CHIPS, TO SERVE

1. In a large bowl, mash the avocados and salt together with a potato masher or large fork until creamy and lump free. Stir in the lime juice, cilantro, and grated onion.
2. In a separate small bowl, press the raspberries with the back of a fork so the fruit is broken down slightly and the juices begin to release. Fold the raspberries into the avocado mixture and serve with tortilla chips.

Avocados provide growing bodies and developing brains with a dose of healthy monounsaturated fats.

The soft and creamy texture of guacamole makes it an ideal snack for baby. You can experiment with spoon-feeding and spreading the dip on soft bread to see what baby likes best.

GF NF Sugar Snap Peas with Honey-Mustard Dip

/ MAKES ABOUT 1 CUP OF DIP /

In the later months of spring, my garden produces an abundance of sugar snap peas, which my boys love to eat right off the vine. When I manage to make it to the kitchen with a few, I enjoy whipping up this sweet, tangy dip. Snap peas aren't the only spring vegetable that can benefit from a dollop of dip—try it on any in-season vegetable. This sauce also works well as a dipping sauce for pretzels, drizzled over salad, as a marinade for chicken and fish, or as a zesty sandwich spread.

½ CUP PLAIN WHOLE-MILK YOGURT
⅓ CUP HONEY
¼ CUP DIJON MUSTARD
BIG PINCH OF KOSHER SALT
2 CUPS FRESH SUGAR SNAP PEAS, WASHED AND TRIMMED

1. To make the dip, simply whisk together the yogurt, honey, mustard, and salt in a medium bowl. Transfer to a serving bowl and serve immediately with sugar snap peas or refrigerate until snack time.

Sugar snap peas contain vitamin B6, which supports bone health.

Quickly blanch sugar snap peas in salted boiling water, cool, and serve plain for a softer, baby-friendly snack. Babies who eat honey will love a drizzle or dip of the sweet sauce on blanched peas.

GF NF DF Pea-Avocado Smoothie

/ MAKES 2 TO 3 GLASSES /

You might feel a bit skeptical after reading over this ingredient list, and I don't blame you. Peas in a smoothie? But the sweetness of the orange juice and the creaminess of the banana more than compensate for the peas and avocado, which means kids get a nice dose of their daily greens without much fuss. Besides, fresh-picked spring peas are often quite sweet on their own. Smoothies are best consumed right after blending, but for on-the-go enjoyment store in a glass jar with a tight-fitting lid, in a cooler or on ice.

1 CUP COOKED PEAS, COOLED

1 CUP ORANGE JUICE

½ AVOCADO

1 BANANA

1 CUP ICE

1. Simply blend all the ingredients in a blender until smooth. Pour into 2 glasses and enjoy.

Peas supply the body with antioxidants, vitamin K, and fiber, which support immunity, bone health, and bowel function.

Smoothies are ideal snacks for baby, as they are smooth, sweet, and packed with health benefits. Depending on your baby's likes, smoothies can be spoon-fed, sipped from a cup through a straw, or frozen into pops for teething relief.

NF Rhubarb-Lemon Biscotti

/ MAKES 4 DOZEN /

Zesty lemon complements sweetened rhubarb in these crumbly, crunchy, citrus-forward cookies. This is a great recipe for curious little cooks, who can try their hand at rolling the dough and shaping the long logs. Biscotti hold up well stored in a lidded glass cookie jar or tightly wrapped in parchment paper. These are especially delicious dipped in ice-cold milk (or coffee, if mom happens to be sneaking a bite!).

1½ CUPS UNBLEACHED ALL-PURPOSE FLOUR
1 CUP SPELT FLOUR
1½ TEASPOONS BAKING POWDER
¼ TEASPOON KOSHER SALT
1 STICK (½ CUP) UNSALTED BUTTER, AT ROOM TEMPERATURE
¾ CUP PURE CANE SUGAR
2 EGGS
1 TEASPOON GRATED LEMON ZEST
1 CUP FINELY DICED RHUBARB (ABOUT 3 STALKS)

1. Preheat the oven to 325°F.
2. Whisk together the flours, baking powder, and salt in a medium bowl. In a large bowl, using an electric mixer, beat the butter and sugar until pale and fluffy, about 3 minutes. Add the eggs one at a time, beating well after each addition. Stir in the lemon zest.
3. With the mixer on low, add a third of the flour mixture to the butter mixture and beat to fully incorporate. Add the rest of the flour mixture in 2 more batches. Add the rhubarb and stir well.
4. Turn out the dough onto a work surface and knead to combine. Divide the dough into 2 equal pieces. On a baking sheet, shape each piece into a log roughly 2 by 14 inches and set them a few inches apart. Bake until light brown, 25 to 30 minutes, then let cool for 10 minutes.
5. Remove the cooled logs from the baking sheet and slice diagonally into ½-inch-thick slices. Arrange the slices flat on the baking sheet and bake for 12 minutes more. Flip the biscotti over and bake again until firm and dry, about 12 more minutes. Let cool. Biscotti wrapped in parchment paper or in a cookie jar on the countertop will keep for up to 3 days.

Rhubarb is chock-full of healthy nutrients, including calcium for strong teeth and bones.

Crisp biscotti are essentially glorified teething biscuits, so let little ones dig in! New teeth and tender gums will love gnawing away on the sweet treat. Just be cautious of big bites—biscotti are hard and can be a choking hazard if baby is not properly monitored while eating.

SUMMER RECIPES

Summer Corn Fritters 100
Grilled Corn on the Cob with Lime Butter 102
Green Smoothie Pops 104
Cherry Tomato Cheddar Bites 105
Melon Slushies 106
Peach Frozen Yogurt 108
Blueberry Baked Oatmeal Cups 110
Grilled Green Beans with Lemony Yogurt Dipping Sauce 114
Bunny Rabbit Rolls 116
Yellow Cherry Tomato and Fresh Mozzarella Pesto Bites 118
Raspberry Lemonade 120
Heat Wave Pops 123
Oven-Dried Stone Fruit 124
Zucchini and Squash Wheels with Marinara Dipping Sauce 126
Zucchini Bread with Honey-Apricot Glaze 128
Peach Olive Oil Muffins 130
Blueberry Lassi 133
Raspberry-Lemon Whole Wheat Mini Pancakes 134
Black Bean Cakes 136
Baba Ghanoush 138
Fresh Summer Rolls with Peanut Dipping Sauce 140
Grilled Nectarine Skewers with Toasted Coconut 142
Feta-Cucumber Dip 144
Tomato-Scallion Biscuits 146
Lemon-Glazed Blueberry Donuts 148

Summer

WITH THE RING OF THE LAST SCHOOL BELL, SUMMER VACATION BEGINS IN ALL ITS GLORY. FOR CHILDREN—AND FOOD LOVERS OF ALL AGES—SUMMER IS A SEASON OF BOUNTIFUL DELIGHT: PEACHES, BERRIES, SWEET CORN, TOMATOES, ICE POPS, PICNICS, BARBECUES, and bonfires. Summer's harvest leaves our bellies full and our taste buds tingling with satisfaction. Seeing as Sarah and I both live a stone's throw from the ocean and beautiful farmland, we might be a bit biased in our fondness for summer. But what's not to love?

If there is one truth we stand by, it's that summer snacks are meant to be eaten outdoors. I love seeing the boys play in the sprinkler with Peach Frozen Yogurt (page 108) running down their little hands and chins. Grilled Corn on the Cob with Lime Butter (page 102) is the perfect summery treat to nibble at the beach as the sun sets. A cooler of Heat Wave Pops (page 123) will be the most popular snack at the pool, and Blueberry Baked Oatmeal Cups (page 110) are the perfect morning treat while rushing out the door to greet a beautiful summer morning.

My favorite Saturday morning ritual is a family walk to our local farmers' market. We forgo breakfast and instead feast on the fresh produce and artisan baked goods available from our favorite vendors. I like to arrive early, as the good stuff tends to go quickly, especially the crowd favorites: peaches, plums, raspberries, nectarines, melons, sweet corn, and heirloom tomatoes. We always run into friends and end up watching our kids run wild at the playground abutting the market.

Seek out your local market and pay it a visit during the height of summer. The abundance will be astounding—each booth piled high with the bountiful harvest of the summer season. The colors and scents are simply divine. Take your kids along, and encourage them to pick out their favorite produce or maybe something completely new and different to take home for tasting. Encourage them to try different varieties of their favorite veggies and fruits—purple peppers, green tomatoes, and white carrots are interesting delicacies.

Another reason to adore summer: it's definitely the most social of the seasons. Backyard cookouts, baseball games, and picnics call for fun, stress-free, nutritious snacks that celebrate the season. I don't want to waste precious summer evenings sweating over a hot stove, so simple, quick pleasures like Fresh Summer Rolls with Peanut Dipping Sauce (page 140) and Melon Slushies (page 106) are perfect for entertaining during the hot months.

The end of summer is the ideal time to prep and freeze summer produce at its height. Berries, corn kernels, sliced stone fruit, green beans, and diced squash can be frozen for winter snacks, baking, and smoothies. Tomatoes can be canned, dried, or pureed and frozen. Imagine the joy of tasting a bit of summer in February—it's worth the extra bit of work!

FAVORITE SUMMER PRODUCE

APRICOTS	FAVA BEANS	PLUMS
ARTICHOKES	GREEN BEANS	RASPBERRIES
BLACKBERRIES	HONEYDEW	STRAWBERRIES
BLUEBERRIES	KALE	SUMMER SQUASH
CANTALOUPE	MELON	TOMATOES
CORN	NECTARINES	WATERMELON
CUCUMBERS	PEACHES	ZUCCHINI
EGGPLANT	PEPPERS	

NF Summer Corn Fritters

/ MAKES 12 FRITTERS /

Nothing says summer like sweet corn straight from the farm stand. There are so many ways to enjoy it: straight off the cob, in chowders and soups, adorning salads, and sprinkled over fish tacos. But these corn fritters have quickly become a family favorite thanks to their big flavor and crunchy consistency, and they make the perfect hearty snack or side to a light summer dinner.

- 3 EARS OF CORN, HUSKS AND SILK REMOVED
- ½ RED BELL PEPPER, FINELY DICED
- ⅓ CUP WHOLE MILK
- 1 LARGE EGG
- ½ TEASPOON BAKING POWDER
- ½ TEASPOON KOSHER SALT
- ¼ TEASPOON GROUND BLACK PEPPER
- ¼ CUP CORNMEAL
- ¼ CUP PLUS 2 TABLESPOONS UNBLEACHED ALL-PURPOSE FLOUR
- 2 TABLESPOONS VEGETABLE OIL
- SOUR CREAM, FOR SERVING

1. To remove the corn kernels, holding on to the stem end of an ear, cut off the tip, stand the ear on its flat tip in a wide shallow bowl, and slice downward with a sharp knife, cutting along the base of the kernels. Discard the cob. Repeat this process with the remaining ears. To the bowl with the kernels, add the bell pepper, milk, egg, baking powder, salt, and black pepper and stir to mix well. Stir in the cornmeal and flour.
2. Heat 1 tablespoon of the oil in a large cast iron skillet over medium heat. Using a tablespoon measure, spoon dollops of batter onto the pan and fry until golden brown, about 2 to 3 minutes per side. Transfer the fritters to a platter and sprinkle them with salt. Repeat the process with the rest of the batter, adding the remaining 1 tablespoon of oil as needed.
3. Serve with sour cream for dipping. The fritters taste best warm or at room temperature on the day of cooking.

Corn's fiber, B vitamins, and protein profile are associated with better blood-sugar control in both type 1 and type 2 diabetics.

The fritters' soft texture and patty shape are ideal for older babies to hold and eat. Smaller babies can enjoy bite-size pieces.

GF NF Grilled Corn on the Cob with Lime Butter

/ MAKES 12 SNACKS /

My boys love corn on the cob. It's a blast to eat, and it is equally amusing for me to watch their little hands and mouths work together to scrape every kernel of goodness off the cob. Grilling the husked cobs is my favorite way to prepare this summer staple, and when served with a tangy, garlicky lime butter, I can promise there won't be any leftovers.

4 EARS OF CORN, HUSKS AND SILK REMOVED

2 TABLESPOONS EXTRA VIRGIN OLIVE OIL

1 STICK (½ CUP) UNSALTED BUTTER, AT ROOM TEMPERATURE

GRATED ZEST OF 1 LIME

2 TABLESPOONS FRESHLY SQUEEZED LIME JUICE

¼ TEASPOON KOSHER SALT

1 TABLESPOON CHOPPED FRESH CILANTRO

½ GARLIC CLOVE, FINELY CHOPPED

1. Preheat the grill to medium high. Rub the ears of corn with olive oil.
2. To make the lime butter, put the butter in a medium bowl and top with the lime zest, lime juice, salt, cilantro, and garlic. Beat it with a large spoon until it becomes soft and creamy. Scrape the butter mixture onto a sheet of parchment paper and roll into a log. Twist the ends of the wrap to seal. Chill the log in the refrigerator until firm, about 1 hour.
3. Grill the corn for a few minutes per side, rotating often, until the kernels are bright yellow and slightly caramelized.
4. When ready to eat, chop each ear of corn into thirds and roll in lime butter.

The high fiber content of corn promotes healthy digestion, while its phytonutrients provide the body with antioxidant benefits.

Older babies will love to gnaw on an ear of corn, while younger babies can enjoy kernels sliced from the cob. If the lime butter is too strong for your little one, simply brush the grilled corn with olive oil for some added nutrition and flavor.

GF NF DF Green Smoothie Pops

/ MAKES 10 TO 12 POPS /

Smoothies are a great way to sneak in a big dose of healthy greens. The sweetness of coconut milk, mango, bananas, and orange juice tone down the otherwise strong flavor of kale. When frozen into pop form, green smoothies become all the more tempting on a sticky-hot summer's day.

- 1 CUP FULL-FAT COCONUT MILK
- 1 CUP MANGO CHUNKS (FRESH OR FROZEN)
- 2 BANANAS
- 1 CUP FRESHLY SQUEEZED ORANGE JUICE
- 2 CUPS KALE LEAVES, STEMS REMOVED

1. Simply blend all the ingredients until smooth. Carefully pour the smoothie mixture into ice-pop molds and freeze until set, about 2 hours. Run the molds under warm water to remove the pops easily.

Kale is a true powerhouse of nutrition. One of the vegetable's many perks is its sulfur content, which aids liver health.

Smoothies are great snacks for baby, as they are sweet but packed with nutrition. Depending on your baby's likes you can serve a smoothie with a spoon, through a straw, in a sippy cup, or frozen into a pop. Teething babies will love the cold comfort of these pops.

GF NF Cherry Tomato Cheddar Bites

/ MAKES 12 BITES /

I plant tomatoes with wild abandon every spring, easily seduced by the promised beauty of heirloom varieties. Come summer, I am swimming in tomatoes, especially cherry tomatoes, and I can barely find the time to can a batch before the next haul comes through the kitchen. Trust me when I say that a single cherry tomato plant can keep you well stocked throughout the summer months. In fact, you might find yourself wondering what to do with your abundant harvest once you've run out of canning steam. May I suggest scooping out the seeds, filling the hollow with a small chunk of cheddar, and baking the little orbs until they are golden brown and oozing delicious cheesiness? Think of a grilled cheese dipped in tomato soup, but without all the bread bogging it down.

12 CHERRY TOMATOES

ONE 8-OUNCE BLOCK CHEDDAR CHEESE, CUT INTO 12 HALF-INCH CUBES

KOSHER SALT AND GROUND BLACK PEPPER

1. Preheat the oven to 425°F.
2. Slice the top off each cherry tomato and, using a small kitchen spoon, gently scoop out the seeds and membranes and discard. Stuff a cheddar cube into each hollowed-out tomato.
3. Arrange the stuffed tomatoes in small groups tightly packed into the cups of a muffin tin to prevent toppling. Sprinkle the tops with salt and pepper, then bake until browned and crisp, about 20 minutes. Cherry Tomato Cheddar Bites are best eaten warm.

Tomatoes' deep red coloring is associated with lycopene, an antioxidant that eliminates dangerous free radicals that can damage DNA and other fragile cell structures.

Older babies will enjoy a cooked stuffed tomato cooled and chopped into bite-size pieces, but tomatoes will be too acidic for younger infants.

GF NF DF Melon Slushies

/ MAKES 6 GLASSES /

The ultimate refreshing summer drink, this cooler can be made with whatever melon variety happens to be your favorite—watermelon, cantaloupe, or honeydew, to name a few. Simply puree the melon with a bit of agave nectar for sweetness, a twist of lime for kick, and crushed ice. It's just like those corner-store slushies we lusted after as kids, but without the dyes and artificial flavors—nothing but sweetness just the way nature intended it!

- 4 CUPS ROUGHLY CHOPPED MELON
- ¼ CUP FRESHLY SQUEEZED LIME JUICE
- 2 TABLESPOONS AGAVE NECTAR
- 2 CUPS ICE

1. Simply blend all the ingredients in a blender until smooth and slushy. Pour into 6 glasses and enjoy with a spoon or straw.

Most melon varieties have lots of fiber and contain vitamins C and A as well as potassium, an electrolyte crucial for proper hydration.

The sweet fruity flavor and icy refreshment of these melon slushies are sure to please little eaters, especially those who are teething.

GF NF Peach Frozen Yogurt

/ MAKES 1 QUART /

Self-proclaimed ice cream aficionados, Sarah and I refused to rest until this frozen yogurt had the creaminess, sweetness, and flavor that we both crave in cold treats. It turns out, the simpler the recipe, the better. The real flavor comes from market-fresh peaches, the kind that send juice cascading down your chin with every bite.

4 LARGE RIPE PEACHES
½ CUP AGAVE NECTAR
JUICE OF ½ LEMON
2 CUPS PLAIN WHOLE-MILK YOGURT
1½ CUPS HEAVY WHIPPING CREAM

1. Cut the peaches in half and remove the pits, then cut three of the peaches into chunks. Process the peach chunks in a food processor with the agave nectar and lemon juice until smooth. Transfer the peach mixture to a large bowl.
2. Peel and cut the remaining peach into ½-inch dice. Add the diced peach, yogurt, and cream to the peach puree and stir until combined. Transfer the yogurt mixture to an ice cream maker and freeze according to the manufacturer's instructions.
3. If you don't have an ice cream maker, transfer the bowl (metal is best) of yogurt mixture to the freezer. After 1 hour, take out the bowl and beat the yogurt mixture using a handheld mixer until smooth, periodically scraping down the sides of the bowl with a spatula (beating prevents the formation of ice crystals). Return the bowl to the freezer and repeat the process a few more times until the yogurt has reached an ice-cream-like consistency. This will take 5 hours or more, depending on your freezer.
4. Once the yogurt is done, remove it from the freezer and allow it to soften until it becomes just scoopable. Serve immediately or transfer to an airtight container and store in the freezer.

Yogurt is a great food for kids who have sensitive bellies. Live yogurt cultures help prevent constipation and diarrhea, and the culturing process makes yogurt easier to digest than milk.

Peach frozen yogurt is a perfect summer treat for baby. Older infants can spoon-feed the frozen yogurt to themselves, while younger babies can be fed spoonfuls.

GF NF Blueberry Baked Oatmeal Cups

/ MAKES 12 SNACKS /

Oatmeal in a portable form—that's the idea behind these treats. Sweetened with apple sauce and maple syrup and flavored with vanilla and cinnamon, these muffins are a fabulous on-the-go, healthy breakfast option. The combined health benefits of blueberries, old-fashioned rolled oats, and flaxseed also make these treats an antioxidant-loaded, fiber-filled snacking powerhouse.

- 2 EGGS
- 2 TEASPOONS PURE VANILLA EXTRACT
- 2 CUPS UNSWEETENED APPLESAUCE
- 1 BANANA, ROUGHLY MASHED
- 1 CUP FRESH BLUEBERRIES
- ½ CUP PURE MAPLE SYRUP
- 3½ CUPS OLD-FASHIONED ROLLED OATS (GLUTEN-FREE IF YOU WISH)
- 1 TEASPOON KOSHER SALT
- 2 TEASPOONS BAKING POWDER
- ¼ CUP GROUND FLAXSEEDS
- 1 TABLESPOON GROUND CINNAMON
- 1½ CUPS WHOLE MILK

1. Preheat the oven to 350°F and line a 12-cup muffin tin with paper liners.
2. In a large bowl, whisk together the eggs, vanilla, applesauce, banana, blueberries, and maple syrup. Add the oats, salt, baking powder, flaxseed, and cinnamon and stir well, making sure everything is well incorporated. Add the milk and stir to combine.
3. Using an ice cream scoop or large spoon, evenly distribute the batter among the prepared muffin cups. Bake for 30 minutes. Eat the oatmeal cups warm or store in an airtight container for future snacking. These cups are best enjoyed warm or at room temperature. Extra oatmeal cups can be stored in the refrigerator for up to 4 days and reheated in a low oven or sliced in half and toasted.

Oatmeal's antioxidants support heart health in a variety of ways, from lowering bad cholesterol to protecting good cholesterol.

Their soft texture makes this muffiny treat a perfect snack for older babies to hold and eat themselves. Small babies can enjoy bite-size pieces.

FIELD TRIP

/ PICK YOUR OWN /

Summer is a bountiful season, especially for farms that grow berries and stone fruits of all shapes, colors, and sizes. Strawberries are the first berries of the season, with a harvest beginning in May or June, while cherries, raspberries, blueberries, and blackberries all reach their peak around late June or July, even into August, depending on where you live. Why not take a field trip to a berry farm? All berry bushes reach close to the ground, which means they are ideal for little helping hands, and of course a just-picked berry still warm from the sun is indescribably delicious. Berries tend to be heavily sprayed crops, so for the health of your family, do your best to seek out organic u-pick options.

Berries of all kinds freeze well for year-round use in baking, smoothies, and fruit-forward desserts. To prepare berries for freezing, simply wash, dry thoroughly, and spread on a baking sheet in a single layer. Freeze the berries thoroughly on the baking sheet before transferring them to a freezer-safe container for storage. Make sure to trim off strawberry tops and pit cherries before freezing to make them easy to use later.

Stone fruits such as nectarines, peaches, and plums tend to be late-summer fruits. Many orchards welcome families for u-pick during the peak harvest season. When picking stone fruits use your sense of touch to feel for fruit that is ever-so-slightly soft beneath your fingers but not at all mushy; this will ensure you get ready-to-eat fruit. However, you can simply store any harder fruits in a brown paper bag at home to encourage ripening. If you pick an abundance of stone fruit and manage to wrestle a few away from your kids, you can prepare them for freezing. Simply wash the fruits, cut them in half and discard the pit, and slice them, then lay the slices in a single layer on a baking sheet and freeze. Once the slices are frozen solid, transfer them to a freezer-safe container and enjoy stone fruits mixed into your morning oatmeal or blended into smoothies throughout the colder months.

Pick Your Own
Raspberries
Blueberries

GF NF Grilled Green Beans with Lemony Yogurt Dipping Sauce

/ MAKES 6 SNACKS /

Plain green beans can be hard for picky eaters to stomach, yet they are loaded with antioxidants, vitamin C, folate, and carotenoids. Given their numerous health benefits it's worth finding a way to get your kids to embrace these veggies. We've found that grilling the beans and pairing them with a citrusy yogurt dipping sauce helps fussier eaters embrace this health superstar.

1 POUND GREEN BEANS, WASHED AND ENDS TRIMMED
2 TABLESPOONS EXTRA VIRGIN OLIVE OIL
PINCH OF KOSHER SALT

FOR THE LEMONY YOGURT DIPPING SAUCE

1 CUP PLAIN WHOLE-MILK GREEK YOGURT
JUICE OF 1 LEMON
PINCH OF KOSHER SALT
2 TABLESPOONS MINCED CHIVES

1. Preheat the grill or grill pan to medium-high.
2. Toss the green beans, olive oil, and salt in a large bowl. Grill the green beans for a few minutes on each side, rotating often, until they are soft and slightly caramelized. Transfer to a plate.
3. To make the sauce, whisk together the yogurt, lemon juice, and salt. Stir in the minced chives.
4. Serve the beans warm with small bowls of dipping sauce.

Green beans help strengthen the body's immune system with their high antioxidant content.

The long shape of grilled green beans makes them an easy handheld snack for babies, but if your baby has only a few teeth, this can be a tough vegetable to chew. If you prefer, slice grilled beans into bite-size pieces and mash slightly for finger food.

GF NF Bunny Rabbit Rolls

/ MAKES 12 ROLLS /

Ideal for picnic lunches, these rolls make use of summer's abundant veggies and include a variety of tastes and textures: different kinds of crunchiness from the bell pepper, cucumber, carrots, and sunflower seeds, and creaminess thanks to a smear of cream cheese. Easy to pack and great for eating on the go, Bunny Rabbit Rolls also lend themselves well to creativity. If you like a bit of sweetness, add in some shredded apple. If you prefer sophisticated creaminess, layer in a few avocado slices. Experiment and customize your ideal roll, or set up an ingredient bar and let your kids build their own.

- 3 FLOUR TORTILLAS (WE SUGGEST WHOLE WHEAT OR SPROUTED WHEAT OR YOUR FAVORITE GLUTEN-FREE TORTILLA, OR TRY OUR HOMEMADE TORTILLA RECIPE, PAGE 222)
- 1 CUCUMBER
- 1 RED BELL PEPPER
- 2 CARROTS, PEELED
- 6 TABLESPOONS CREAM CHEESE
- 3 TABLESPOONS RAW SUNFLOWER SEEDS
- 1 CUP CHOPPED BABY SPINACH

1. Warm the tortillas slightly in the oven to make them more pliable.
2. Cut the cucumber, red bell pepper, and carrots into thin ribbons using a vegetable peeler or a mandoline. Place all three tortillas on the countertop. Onto each tortilla, spread 2 tablespoons of the cream cheese and sprinkle 1 tablespoon of the sunflower seeds. In the center of each tortilla, arrange ⅓ of the mixed vegetable ribbons and ⅓ cup of the spinach. To create rolls, tuck in two sides of each tortilla and, starting at one end, roll into a tight tube. Place the rolls on a cutting board with their seam sides down. With a sharp knife, slice each roll into 4 portions.

Red bell peppers contain vitamin B6, which is essential to the health of the nervous system and the renewal of cells.

Older babies will enjoy an assembled Bunny Rabbit Roll, while younger babes can eat the sliced vegetable ribbons alongside small pieces of tortilla spread with cream cheese.

GF Yellow Cherry Tomato and Fresh Mozzarella Pesto Bites

/ MAKES 12 SNACKS /

A finger-food version of a caprese salad, these bites pack on the flavor with cherry tomatoes and marinated mozzarella layered on toothpicks. They are perfect for backyard barbecues and picnics. Plan to make more pesto than the recipe calls for: pesto is an ideal summer sauce to have on hand for pasta, pizza, and jazzing up simple grilled vegetable and meats.

- 2 CUPS PACKED FRESH BASIL LEAVES
- 2 GARLIC CLOVES
- ¼ CUP PINE NUTS, TOASTED
- ½ CUP EXTRA VIRGIN OLIVE OIL
- SQUEEZE OF LEMON JUICE
- ⅓ CUP FRESHLY GRATED PECORINO CHEESE
- KOSHER SALT AND GROUND BLACK PEPPER
- 1 CUP CHERRY TOMATOES, SLICED IN HALF
- 1 CUP SMALL FRESH MOZZARELLA BALLS (BOCCONCINI), SLICED IN HALF
- 12 WOODEN TOOTHPICKS

1. To make the pesto, process the basil, garlic, and pine nuts in a food processor until they form a fine paste. With the motor running, stream in the olive oil and lemon juice. Pour the pesto into a large bowl and stir in the Pecorino cheese. Add salt and pepper to taste. Transfer to small dipping bowls for serving. Pesto is best stored in an airtight glass container and should be enjoyed within 2 weeks. It tastes best at room temperature.
2. Toss the halved tomatoes and mozzarella balls in the pesto to coat evenly. Skewer the tomatoes and cheese on wooden toothpicks, alternating between the two. Lay the skewers on a tray to serve immediately with the pesto or store in a glass container in the refrigerator for up to 2 days.

Basil's aromatic compound, terpenoids, makes this herb a health all-star. Basil acts as a diuretic to help the body expel unwanted toxins and supports the functioning of the kidneys. It is also good for digestive health and overall detoxifying.

Simply slice tomatoes and mozzarella into small pieces for a baby-friendly snack. If your infant has experience with pine nuts, toss small slices in pesto for extra flavor and nutrition.

GF NF DF Raspberry Lemonade

/ MAKES 4 TO 6 GLASSES /

Down a windy path behind Sarah's childhood home, a patch of thorny raspberry bushes grows with wild abandon. At the height of summer, Sarah visits the bushes weekly with her boys in tow, eagerly awaiting the berries' turn from blush to deep reds and purples. At the peak of ripeness, Sarah and her boys fill their baskets full, return to the kitchen, and revel in the first refreshing sip of Raspberry Lemonade. This recipe relies on the simplicity of freshly squeezed lemons and agave nectar, and adds a kick of fruitiness in the form of raspberry sauce. Free of artificial dyes and sugars, the gorgeous natural pink color makes it even more fun to sip.

½ CUP AGAVE NECTAR
5 CUPS PLUS 1 TABLESPOON COLD WATER
½ CUP FRESH RASPBERRIES, PLUS MORE FOR SERVING
1 CUP FRESHLY SQUEEZED LEMON JUICE (FROM 4 TO 6 LEMONS)
1 LEMON, SLICED THIN, FOR SERVING

1. Make a simple syrup by heating the agave and 1 cup of the water in a small saucepan until the agave is dissolved completely. Set aside to cool.
2. Make a raspberry sauce by processing the raspberries and 1 tablespoon of the water in a food processor until the raspberries form a smooth puree, then transfer the puree to a fine-mesh strainer over a bowl. Using a spatula, press the puree through the strainer to create a smooth sauce. Discard the seeds that remain in the strainer.
3. Pour the lemon juice and simple syrup into a pitcher, then add the remaining 4 cups of water. Stir in the prepared raspberry sauce and refrigerate for 30 to 40 minutes. When ready to serve, fill cups with ice, pour in the raspberry lemonade, and top with a few fresh raspberries and thin slices of lemon.

Lemons are a good source of electrolytes such as potassium, calcium, and magnesium, which help hydrate the body and regulate its functioning.

Baby can enjoy a few raspberries or even suck on a lemon slice while the older children and adults sip lemonade. Juice is not recommended for babies because of its high sugar content; water is sufficient for hydration.

GF NF DF Heat Wave Pops

/ MAKES 6 TO 10 POPS /

Growing up, Sarah and her sister would pass hot summer days on Martha's Vineyard by experimenting in the kitchen. These fruity ice pops are a nod to their favorite "recipe" of filling ice-pop molds with orange juice—simple but perfectly delicious. Heat Wave Pops offer a bit more nutritional value, combining coconut water with whole berries. Loaded with electrolytes and potassium, coconut water is ideal for rehydration, and during the summer months—with kids spending more time in the sun working up a sweat—hydration is critical.

2 CUPS COCONUT WATER
½ CUP BLUEBERRIES
½ CUP RASPBERRIES OR BLACKBERRIES

1. Drop a mixture of berries into the bottoms of empty ice-pop molds or small waxed-paper cups, distributing them evenly among the molds. Carefully pour coconut water over the berries and insert ice-pop sticks. Allow the pops to freeze until set, about 2 hours. Loosen by quickly running the molds under warm water.

Blackberry's rich blue color indicates that the fruit contains high levels of ellagic acid, a powerful antioxidant. Additionally, the high tannin content of blackberries offers a wide variety of digestive health benefits including the reduction of intestinal inflammation.

Babies will love the sweet and refreshing taste of coconut water and berry ice pops. Smaller babies can share licks of yours, while older infants will enjoy holding their own.

GF NF DF Oven-Dried Stone Fruit

/ MAKES 2 CUPS /

Our recipe for Oven-Dried Stone Fruit is simply pure fruit sliced into bite-size pieces and dehydrated in the oven at a low temperature for 4 hours. Packed in reusable snack bags, these travel well, and they are a personal favorite for road trips and long plane rides. Healthy, sweet, and easy to eat!

4 RIPE PEACHES

4 RIPE PLUMS

4 RIPE APRICOTS

1. Preheat the oven to 200°F. Line a baking sheet with parchment paper and top with a wire rack.
2. Cut the fruits in half and remove the pits. Cut the flesh into ¼-inch slices. Evenly arrange the fruit slices on the wire rack and bake in the oven for 4 hours. The intoxicating smell will force you to try a bite right out of the oven, but the remaining dried fruit can be stored in airtight containers for up to 2 weeks.

Peaches contain a high dose of vitamins A and C, which are crucial for the maintenance of healthy skin. This stone fruit is also rich in fiber, which aids in digestion and makes for a satiating snack.

Older babies will enjoy holding a whole slice of oven-dried fruit and chewing on the soft flesh, while younger infants will benefit from smaller pieces.

NF Zucchini and Squash Wheels with Marinara Dipping Sauce

/ MAKES ABOUT 2 DOZEN WHEELS /

As addictive as potato chips, these zucchini rounds are crunchy and cheesy, thanks to a roll in nutty Parmesan cheese and panko bread crumbs. Dipped in your favorite marinara sauce they become a bold and satisfying snack choice, perfect for a movie marathon on a rainy summer's day, as an easy dinner side dish, or for feeding the hungry masses after a morning spent running around the playground.

- 1 TABLESPOON EXTRA VIRGIN OLIVE OIL
- 1 ZUCCHINI
- 1 SUMMER SQUASH
- 1 TEASPOON KOSHER SALT
- 1 CUP UNBLEACHED ALL-PURPOSE FLOUR
- 1 CUP PANKO BREAD CRUMBS
- 1 CUP FRESHLY GRATED PARMESAN CHEESE
- 3 EGGS
- 1 CUP MARINARA SAUCE (YOUR FAVORITE), FOR DIPPING

1. Preheat the oven to 425°F. Brush a wire rack with some of the olive oil and place it on a baking sheet.
2. Trim the ends off the zucchini and summer squash and slice into ⅛-inch wheels. Put slices in a sieve, sprinkle with the salt, and toss with the flour, shaking off excess.
3. In a shallow bowl, combine the bread crumbs and Parmesan cheese. Whisk the eggs in another shallow bowl. One by one, dip the wheels first into the egg wash and then into bread crumb mixture, patting it on so it sticks. Arrange the wheels on the oiled rack in a single layer. Brush the tops with olive oil. Bake for 20 to 30 minutes, until the bread crumbs are golden. Meanwhile, warm up the marinara sauce. Serve the squash wheels with a cup of warm marinara sauce for dipping.

Zucchini's vitamin C aids the immune and respiratory systems, while the vegetable's vitamin A promotes healthy eyes, skin, and liver function.

The small, round shape of these snack wheels makes them a perfect veggie treat for baby to hold and munch on. For an easy finger food for younger babies, chop the wheels into small bites and lightly mash.

DF Zucchini Bread with Honey-Apricot Glaze

/ MAKES 2 LOAVES OR 24 MUFFINS /

All vegetable gardeners are familiar with the zucchini conundrum. Come late summer, giant zucchini spring forth from their vines and demand your attention. After grilling them, shredding them into omelets, and slicing them into veggie lasagna, I'm always left with more, wondering how I'll possibly use them up before they turn. Why not try baking shredded zucchini into a sweet, nutty treat topped with a golden apricot glaze?

FOR THE BREAD

3 EGGS
1 CUP EXTRA VIRGIN OLIVE OIL
1 CUP HONEY
2 CUPS GRATED ZUCCHINI
2 TEASPOONS PURE VANILLA EXTRACT
3 CUPS UNBLEACHED ALL-PURPOSE FLOUR
1 TABLESPOON GROUND CINNAMON
1 TEASPOON BAKING SODA
½ TEASPOON BAKING POWDER
1 TEASPOON KOSHER SALT
½ CUP CHOPPED WALNUTS
1 CUP RAISINS

1. Preheat the oven to 350°F. Generously grease and flour two 8 × 4-inch loaf pans or two muffin tins.
2. To make the bread, whisk the eggs in a large bowl, then stir in the olive oil, honey, zucchini, and vanilla. In a medium bowl, stir together the flour, cinnamon, baking soda, baking powder, salt, walnuts, and raisins. Add the flour mixture to the egg mixture and stir until just combined. Carefully divide the batter between the prepared loaf pans or among the muffin cups. Bake loaves for 30 to 40 minutes or bake muffins for 20 to 25 minutes, until a toothpick inserted into the center comes out clean. Let cool in the pans on a wire rack for 10 minutes and then remove from the pans to cool completely.
3. While the bread is baking, make the glaze: Process the apricots and honey in a food processor until smooth. Pour the apricot-honey mixture into a small saucepan, bring it to a boil, reduce the heat, and simmer until slightly thickened, about 3 minutes. Set aside to cool slightly.

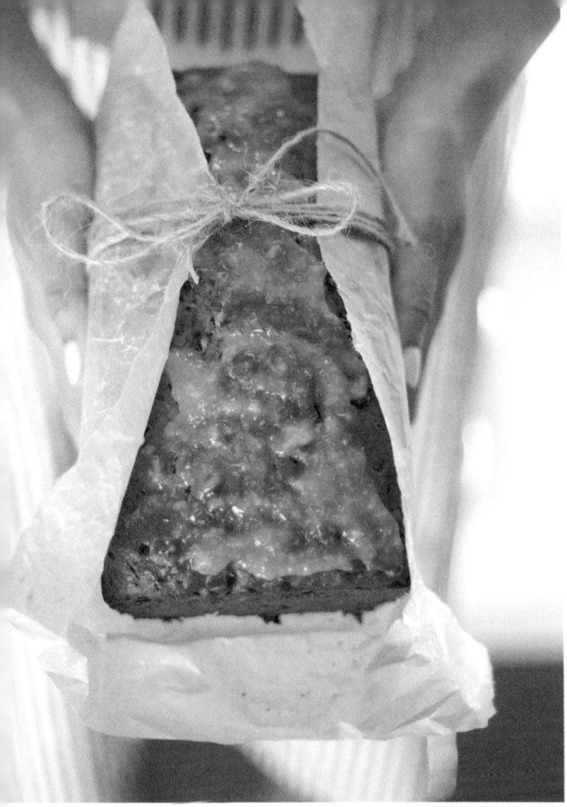

FOR THE GLAZE

2 VERY RIPE APRICOTS, PITTED

2 TABLESPOONS HONEY

4. When the loaves or muffins are cool, spoon the glaze over the top. Let the glaze set before cutting. The bread will keep sealed in an airtight container or wrapped tightly in parchment paper or beeswax wrap on the countertop for up to 3 days. It tastes best reheated in a low oven or sliced and toasted.

Apricots' abundant beta-carotene makes them a heart-healthy choice, their vitamin A promotes healthy vision, and their high fiber content aids in healthy digestion.

Babies of all ages will enjoy this soft, sweet bread. For younger infants who have yet to try walnuts, simply omit them from the batter.

NF DF Peach Olive Oil Muffins

/ MAKES 12 MUFFINS /

Baking with olive oil adds density, depth, and just a whisper of savory flavor. With ripe, juicy peaches and a hint of vanilla, these olive oil muffins are perfectly sweet without being over the top. We suggest serving them with a dollop of Greek yogurt, which adds just a little creaminess to the finish. They're also amazing served hot with a pat of butter.

- 3 RIPE PEACHES, PITTED AND CUT INTO THIN SLICES
- 1½ CUPS EXTRA VIRGIN OLIVE OIL
- ½ CUP PURE MAPLE SYRUP
- ½ TEASPOON KOSHER SALT
- 3 LARGE EGGS
- 1 TEASPOON PURE VANILLA EXTRACT
- 1 CUP UNBLEACHED ALL-PURPOSE FLOUR
- 1 CUP WHOLE WHEAT FLOUR
- ½ CUP PACKED DARK BROWN SUGAR
- ½ TEASPOON BAKING POWDER
- ½ TEASPOON BAKING SODA
- 1 CUP PLAIN WHOLE-MILK GREEK YOGURT, FOR SERVING (OPTIONAL; OMIT FOR DAIRY-FREE VERSION)

1. Preheat the oven to 350°F and line a 12-cup muffin tin with paper liners.
2. In a large bowl, toss the peaches with ¼ cup of the olive oil, ¼ cup of the maple syrup, and the salt. Let them stand until juicy, about 15 minutes. In a medium bowl, whisk together the eggs, vanilla, and the remaining 1¼ cups of olive oil and ¼ cup of maple syrup. In a third bowl, whisk together the flours, sugar, baking powder, and baking soda. Add the flour mixture to the egg mixture, then fold in the peaches with their juices.
3. Using an ice cream scoop or large spoon, evenly distribute the batter among the prepared muffin cups. Bake for 20 to 25 minutes, until golden and a toothpick inserted into the center of a muffin comes out clean. Let the muffins cool slightly, then serve with a dollop of Greek yogurt. Muffins will keep sealed in an airtight container on the countertop for 3 days, and they taste best reheated in a low oven or sliced in half and toasted.

Olive oil supports many of the body's important functions, from digestion to bone health to cognition.

Muffins are an ideal snack for babies to feed to themselves. For younger babies, mash muffin crumbs into yogurt for a spoon-fed snack, or crumble up a muffin for an easy finger food.

GF NF Blueberry Lassi

/ MAKES 4 GLASSES /

I'll never forget the first time we took Vijay, my eldest son, out for Indian food. Given that he's half-Indian, my husband and I were hopeful that he would embrace the culinary world of chutney and curry. He greedily shoveled in mouthfuls of chicken tikka masala and black dal before the spiciness caught up with him. Happily, a lassi helped to alleviate the spicy sting, and he's been a fan of Indian food (and drink) ever since. Cool and creamy with a hint of blueberry, this lassi is refreshing and filling, thanks to a base of whole-milk yogurt. Plain yogurt can be an acquired taste for little ones who are used to highly sweetened fruit-flavored yogurt. You might try adding a bit more agave if that's the case.

- 2 CUPS FRESH BLUEBERRIES, PLUS MORE FOR TOPPING
- 2 CUPS PLAIN WHOLE-MILK YOGURT
- ¼ CUP AGAVE NECTAR
- 1 CUP ICE

1. Simply blend all the ingredients in a blender until smooth. Pour into 4 glasses and top with a few fresh blueberries and a straw for sipping.

Blueberries' deep blue color indicates the presence of antioxidant nutrients, which improve cognitive function and support eye health and the cardiovascular system.

A blueberry lassi is sure to satisfy baby with its creamy, sweet taste. Depending on your infant's age, try serving a lassi with a spoon, through a straw, or in a sippy cup.

NF Raspberry-Lemon Whole Wheat Mini Pancakes

/ MAKES ABOUT 2 DOZEN /

These pancakes are so light they just about float off the plate and into your mouth, and once they hit your taste buds, the combination of lemon and raspberry will convince you they are the perfect summery breakfast. When the seasons begin to change, experiment with the additions. Sautéed apples or pumpkin puree is fabulous in the fall, and dried cranberries and pecans are a favorite wintertime pairing. For an extra-special weekend breakfast treat, my boys love when I mix in chocolate chips, toasted pecans, and shredded coconut.

1 CUP WHOLE WHEAT FLOUR
2/3 CUP UNBLEACHED ALL-PURPOSE FLOUR
1/3 CUP TOASTED WHEAT GERM
1 TEASPOON BAKING POWDER
½ TEASPOON BAKING SODA
¼ TEASPOON KOSHER SALT
GRATED ZEST OF 1 LEMON
3 TABLESPOONS UNSALTED BUTTER, MELTED, PLUS MORE FOR THE GRIDDLE
2¾ CUPS LOW-FAT BUTTERMILK
2 LARGE EGGS, LIGHTLY BEATEN
1 TABLESPOON AGAVE NECTAR
1½ CUP FRESH RASPBERRIES, PLUS MORE FOR SERVING
PURE MAPLE SYRUP, FOR SERVING

1. Heat a griddle or cast iron skillet over medium heat.
2. Whisk together the flours, wheat germ, baking powder, baking soda, salt, and lemon zest in a medium bowl and set aside. In a large bowl, whisk together the melted butter, buttermilk, eggs, and agave. Add the flour mixture to the buttermilk mixture and stir until just combined. The batter will be slightly lumpy.
3. Coat the griddle with butter. Working in batches and using a tablespoon measure, spoon dollops of batter onto the griddle, then dot with a few raspberries. Cook until the surface is bubbling and edges start to set up, 2 to 3 minutes. Flip the pancakes and cook until the undersides are golden brown, 2 to 3 minutes more. Serve mini pancakes with maple syrup and more raspberries, if desired. Extra pancakes can easily be frozen and popped into the toaster for a quick breakfast.

Raspberries are packed with fiber, which helps to keep the gastrointestinal system flowing smoothly, and vitamin C, which promotes a healthy immune system.

The soft texture and petite size of these pancakes make them an easy handheld treat for baby. Smaller babies will enjoy bite-size pieces.

NF DF Black Bean Cakes

/ MAKES 12 TO 15 SMALL CAKES /

Humble rice and beans dressed up with a variety of toppings is a favorite meal at Sarah's house, and these multitasking black bean cakes are a fun spin on the classic pairing. Their heartiness is due to the combination of millet, black beans, and corn, while the flavor kick comes from a pinch of chili powder, cumin, and garlic. While sliced avocado is a perfect accompaniment, you might also try sandwiching them on a bun with juicy tomato slices, fresh lettuce, and a smear of spicy mustard or mayonnaise. This snack can carry kids through to any meal.

- ½ CUP UNCOOKED MILLET
- 3 TABLESPOONS EXTRA VIRGIN OLIVE OIL
- 1 CUP WATER
- 2½ CUPS COOKED BLACK BEANS (ABOUT 1¾ CANS, DRAINED AND RINSED)
- ½ CUP BREAD CRUMBS
- ½ SMALL ONION, CHOPPED FINE
- 2 GARLIC CLOVES, MINCED
- 1 TEASPOON CHILI POWDER
- 1 TEASPOON GROUND CUMIN

1. In a small saucepan over medium heat, toast the millet in 1 tablespoon of the olive oil for a few minutes. Add the water and a pinch of salt and bring to a boil. Reduce the heat to low, cover, and cook until the water is absorbed, about 15 minutes.
2. Put the black beans, cooked millet, bread crumbs, onion, garlic, chili powder, cumin, tomato paste, corn, egg, cilantro, and salt into a large bowl. Mix everything together with your hands until well combined.
3. Heat a cast iron skillet over medium-high heat. Divide the black bean mixture into golf-ball-size pieces, then use your hands to form small patties. Drizzle enough of the remaining 2 tablespoons of olive oil to cover the bottom of the pan. Cook the patties in batches until they are deep brown and crisp, about

1 TABLESPOON TOMATO PASTE

½ CUP CORN KERNELS

1 EGG

¼ CUP CHOPPED FRESH CILANTRO

1 TEASPOON KOSHER SALT

1 AVOCADO, SLICED, FOR SERVING

5 minutes on each side. Add more olive oil as needed. Serve the cakes immediately. To store extra cakes, layer them between sheets of parchment paper and place them in an airtight glass container. They will keep in the refrigerator for up to 4 days.

Black beans are rich in both protein and fiber, which help to steady the digestive process.

Crumble a black bean cake into finger food for baby or spoon-feed small pieces.

GF NF DF Baba Ghanoush

/ MAKES 2 CUPS /

Eggplant can be hard for young palates to embrace, but this creamy dip offers a gentle introduction to the gorgeous, fiber-packed purple veggie. Tahini gives this dip its creaminess, while garlic, lemon, and a pinch of cumin offer a pop of sophisticated flavor. This dip is perfect served with crusty bread and crispy vegetables.

- 1 LARGE EGGPLANT
- ¼ CUP TAHINI
- 2 GARLIC CLOVES, MINCED
- ¼ CUP FRESHLY SQUEEZED LEMON JUICE
- PINCH OF GROUND CUMIN
- BIG PINCH OF KOSHER SALT
- 3 TABLESPOONS EXTRA VIRGIN OLIVE OIL
- 1 TABLESPOON CHOPPED FRESH FLAT-LEAF PARSLEY
- 1 TABLESPOON CHOPPED FRESH MINT
- CRUSTY BREAD, FOR SERVING (USE GLUTEN-FREE BREAD OR CRACKERS IF YOU WISH)
- ASSORTED FRESH VEGETABLES, FOR SERVING

1. Preheat the grill to medium-high and preheat the oven to 375°F.
2. Prick the eggplant all over with a fork and grill, turning frequently, until the skin blackens and the vegetable softens, 15 to 20 minutes. Transfer the eggplant to a baking sheet and bake in the oven until very soft, about 20 more minutes. Let the eggplant cool in the pan until you can comfortably handle it. Peel off the skin and discard.
3. Transfer the eggplant flesh into a medium bowl and mash with a fork. To the eggplant paste, add the tahini, garlic, lemon juice, cumin, salt, and 2 tablespoons of the olive oil. Stir well and adjust seasoning to taste.
4. Scoop the Baba Ghanoush into a serving bowl and, with the back of a spoon, form a shallow well. Pour the remaining 1 tablespoon of olive oil and sprinkle with the parsley and mint. Enjoy at room temperature with bread and fresh vegetables. Baba Ghanoush will keep sealed in a glass container in the refrigerator for about 4 days.

Eggplant has a high fiber content, which helps the digestive process. Given this vegetable's rich purple hue, it comes as no surprise that it is also a good source of antioxidants.

Babies may enjoy spoonfuls of Baba Ghanoush or like the dip spread onto soft bread.

GF DF Fresh Summer Rolls with Peanut Dipping Sauce

/ MAKES 7 ROLLS /

These rolls make the best kind of picnic food—not to mention a lunch-box staple for fall—with crunchy scallions, fresh herbs, creamy avocado, irresistible peanut dipping sauce, and no soggy sandwich bread. The peanut sauce is perhaps the very best part, equally sweet and savory, creamy and tangy. Make a double batch to have extra on hand for dipping vegetables in and to marinate chicken, fish, and veggies for the grill. If you aren't a fan of tofu (there is some debate over the healthiness of soy-based products such as tofu, especially given the fact it often contains GMOs), simply omit the tofu and ramp up the avocado with a pinch of curry powder!

FOR THE ROLLS

4 OUNCES ¼-INCH-THICK THAI RICE NOODLES
BOILING WATER
½ POUND EXTRA-FIRM TOFU
1 TEASPOON CURRY POWDER
PINCH OF KOSHER SALT
7 RICE PAPER WRAPPERS (ALSO KNOWN AS SPRING ROLL SKINS OR BÁNG TRÁNG)
2 AVOCADOS, SLICED
1 CUP CHOPPED FRESH MINT
1 CUP CHOPPED SCALLIONS
1 CUP CHOPPED FRESH CILANTRO

1. To make the rolls, first hydrate the rice noodles: Place the dry noodles in a large bowl, then pour hot water over the noodles to cover. Place a lid on the bowl and let the noodles sit until soft, about 10 minutes.
2. In a medium bowl, crumble up the tofu with your fingers. Add the curry powder and salt and toss until the tofu forms clumps the size of peas.
3. To prepare the rice paper wrappers, heat a kettle of water and pour the hot water into a large shallow dish. Carefully dip a rice paper wrapper into the water for about 15 seconds, until soft. Place the soft wrapper on a work surface and onto the bottom third of the wrapper layer small amounts of the noodles, tofu mixture, avocado, mint, scallions, and cilantro, leaving some space on both sides. Wrap the edge closest to the filling over the filling firmly, fold in both sides, and continue to roll up until the roll is neatly closed. Repeat the process to build 6 more rolls.

FOR THE SAUCE

½ CUP SMOOTH PEANUT BUTTER

½ CUP COCONUT MILK

¼ CUP LOW-SODIUM SOY SAUCE

1 TEASPOON AGAVE NECTAR

SQUEEZE OF LIME JUICE

4. To make the sauce, simply whisk together all the sauce ingredients or blend in a blender. Slice the rolls in half and serve with a small bowl of peanut dipping sauce.
5. To store, wrap each roll in a damp paper towel. Place all the wrapped rolls in an airtight container and store in the refrigerator. Eat within 2 days. The peanut sauce can be kept in a glass jar in the refrigerator for up to a week.

Avocados provide growing bodies with an important dose of fiber to help keep the digestive system moving.

Make up a plate of spring roll fillings for baby to snack on: a small pile of finely chopped noodles, crumbled plain tofu, and sliced avocado. The rolls themselves are too difficult for babies to bite and chew.

GF NF DF Grilled Nectarine Skewers with Toasted Coconut

/ MAKES 6 SNACKS /

I love fruit-forward dessert dishes during the summer months when berries and stone fruits are at their peak. Crumbles, pies, cobblers, and shortcakes are the best for showcasing summer's bounty. The idea of grilling fruit was new to me, but this easy technique has quickly worked its way into my dessert repertoire. Using skewers to grill the nectarine pieces turns this sweet treat into an easy-to-eat finger food and makes the grilling process simple. Enjoy with a brush of honey and rolled in nutty toasted coconut.

- 1 CUP UNSWEETENED SHREDDED COCONUT
- 3 NECTARINES
- 2 TABLESPOONS EXTRA VIRGIN OLIVE OIL
- 3 TABLESPOONS HONEY

1. Heat the grill or grill pan to medium-high.
2. Toast the coconut in a dry skillet over medium heat until lightly browned and set aside.
3. Slice the nectarines in half, discard the pits, and then chop into 1-inch cubes. Toss in a medium bowl with the olive oil to evenly coat, then string onto wooden skewers. Set the assembled skewers on the grill and brush the nectarines with the honey. Grill for about 3 minutes, until the fruit is caramelized and grill marks appear. Continue to cook, rotating the skewers and brushing each side with honey, until evenly caramelized, about 3 minutes more. Roll the grilled skewers in the toasted coconut, then lay on a platter for serving.

Given its beautiful orange hue, it's no surprise that the nectarine is a great source of beta-carotene, which the body converts into vitamin A, essential for building and maintaining healthy skin, teeth, bone tissue, soft tissue, and mucous membranes.

Babies who enjoy honey can snack on thin slices of grilled nectarine with toasted coconut. If your child isn't eating honey yet, simply omit it or replace with agave nectar. Younger babies will enjoy plain mashed grilled nectarines mixed into yogurt or oatmeal.

GF NF Feta-Cucumber Dip

/ MAKES 2 CUPS OF DIP /

I love setting out a bowl of healthy dip along with a tempting array of *crudités*, pita chips, and crackers. The boys flock to the table on their own, and although they start with the chips and crackers, before long they're digging into the vegetables too. I'm a big believer in using the art of display to tempt my boys to the healthy side. This dip, with its creamy feta and Greek-yogurt base and sprinkling of dill, is a big help in my tempting efforts.

1 MEDIUM CUCUMBER, PEELED

¼ TEASPOON KOSHER SALT

1 CUP PLAIN WHOLE-MILK GREEK YOGURT

½ CUP CRUMBLED FETA CHEESE

¼ CUP FINELY CHOPPED FRESH DILL

¼ CUP HEAVY CREAM

JUICE OF ½ LEMON

PINCH OF GROUND BLACK PEPPER

PITA CHIPS, TO SERVE (USE GLUTEN-FREE BREAD OR CRACKERS IF YOU WISH)

SLICED VEGETABLES, TO SERVE

1. Cut the cucumber in half lengthwise, scoop out the seeds, and grate the flesh on the large holes of a box grater. Wrap the grated cucumber in a clean kitchen towel and squeeze out the excess water.
2. In a medium bowl, stir together the grated cucumber, salt, yogurt, feta cheese, dill, cream, lemon juice, and pepper. Add additional salt and pepper to taste. Transfer to a serving bowl and serve with pita chips or sliced vegetables for dipping. Feta-Cucumber Dip keeps well in an airtight container in the refrigerator for up to 3 days.

Cucumbers are 95 percent water, keeping the body hydrated while helping to eliminate harmful toxins.

The soft and creamy texture of this dip makes an easy snack for baby. Infants will enjoy it off a spoon or spread onto soft bread.

NF Tomato-Scallion Biscuits

/ MAKES 10 TO 12 BISCUITS /

I've always envied Southern-born cooks who have the perfect biscuit recipe up their sleeve, always at the ready to impress brunch or dinner crowds. Alas, as a Midwesterner by birth, I've been on the hunt for an "heirloom" recipe of my own—that is, I was until Sarah pulled a tray of these beauties out of the oven! The combination of scallions and tomato gives these light, moist biscuits an intense savory flavor. Although they're a hearty snack on their own, they also make for an incredible base for breakfast sandwiches.

- 2 CUPS UNBLEACHED ALL-PURPOSE FLOUR
- 3½ TEASPOONS BAKING POWDER
- ½ TEASPOON KOSHER SALT
- ½ TEASPOON CREAM OF TARTAR
- 1 STICK (½ CUP) COLD BUTTER, CUT INTO SMALL CUBES
- ⅔ CUP PLUS 3 TABLESPOONS WHOLE MILK
- 1 TABLESPOON HONEY
- 1 CUP QUARTERED CHERRY TOMATOES
- ¼ CUP THINLY SLICED SCALLIONS

1. Preheat the oven to 450°F and line a baking sheet with parchment paper.
2. Put the flour, baking powder, salt, and cream of tartar into a food processor and whiz to combine. Add the butter and pulse until pea-size clumps form. Transfer the flour mixture to a medium-size bowl and add ⅔ cup of the milk and the honey, tomatoes, and scallions. Stir to combine.
3. Transfer the dough onto a floured surface and knead about 10 times with well-floured hands. Roll the dough into a slab about ¾-inch thick. Using a biscuit cutter or the rim of a drinking glass, cut out circles of dough.
4. Arrange the dough circles an inch apart on the baking sheet. Brush the tops with the remaining 3 tablespoons of milk. Bake for about 10 minutes, until golden brown, then let them rest for 10 minutes before enjoying. Cooled biscuits will keep sealed in an airtight container on the countertop for up to 3 days. To reheat, warm the biscuits in a low oven or slice in half and toast for best results.

The rich supply of antioxidants in tomatoes supports bone health and offers anticancer benefits.

Older infants will be happy holding and munching on a whole biscuit, while younger babies can snack on crumbs.

Lemon-Glazed Blueberry Donuts

/ MAKES 6 LARGE DONUTS /

No kid-friendly cookbook is complete without a donut recipe, even this health-conscious book of ours. These baked donuts have a slightly chewy texture thanks to the almond meal, as well as fruit-forward flavor thanks to applesauce and farm-fresh blueberries. While many donuts are over-the-top sweet, ours have a mild sweetness. Lemony glaze, with its refreshingly sweet tang, is the perfect topping. You'll need a special donut pan to get the classic donut shape.

FOR THE DONUTS

1 CUP UNBLEACHED ALL-PURPOSE FLOUR

⅓ CUP PURE CANE SUGAR

¼ CUP ALMOND MEAL

1 TEASPOON BAKING POWDER

½ TEASPOON KOSHER SALT

2 EGGS

¼ CUP PLUS 3 TABLESPOONS BUTTERMILK

3 TABLESPOONS UNSWEETENED APPLESAUCE

2 TABLESPOONS EXTRA VIRGIN COCONUT OIL, MELTED

2 TEASPOONS PURE VANILLA EXTRACT

⅓ CUP FRESH BLUEBERRIES

1. Preheat the oven to 350°F. If your donut pan is not nonstick, grease the surface with a bit of canola oil or melted coconut oil.
2. To make the donuts, whisk together the flour, sugar, almond meal, baking powder, and salt in a medium bowl. (If you can't find prepared almond meal, simply whiz raw almonds in a food processor until they reach a sandy consistency.) In a large bowl, whisk together the eggs, buttermilk, applesauce, coconut oil, and vanilla, then stir in the blueberries. Add the flour mixture to the blueberry mixture and stir gently until just combined.
3. Pour the batter into the donut pan, filling each mold to the top, and bake for 20 minutes, until the center is set and the edges are just beginning to brown. Let the donuts cool in the pan for 5 minutes, then transfer to a wire rack to finish cooling.
4. While the donuts bake, make the glaze: Whisk together the sugar, cream, and lemon juice. Don't overwhisk the glaze or it will become too thick. (If this happens, however, don't panic—you can always thin it out with extra cream and lemon juice.)

FOR THE GLAZE

1 CUP POWDERED SUGAR

3 TABLESPOONS HEAVY CREAM

3 TABLESPOONS FRESHLY SQUEEZED LEMON JUICE

5. Place a wire rack on a baking sheet to catch drips. Dip one side of each cooled donut into the glaze, rotating to coat the top, then lay, glazed side up, on the wire rack. Repeat until all the donuts have been glazed. Allow the glaze to set. Prepared donuts will keep wrapped in parchment paper or beeswax wrap on the countertop for up to 3 days.

Blueberries offer a wide variety of antioxidant nutrients, which support the cardiovascular system and improve cognitive function.

Babies who enjoy nuts will love to snack on bits of crumbled donut. Infants yet to eat nuts can simply snack on a few mashed berries on their own or mixed into a favorite food. A donut's round shape makes it an ideal handheld treat for older babies.

FALL RECIPES

Cranberry-Orange Buttermilk Snacking Cake 154
Caramel Apples with Sea Salt 156
Brussels Sprout Crisps with Parmesan and Lemon 160
Kale Chips with Butternut Squash Seed Oil and Sea Salt 162
Baked Apple Chips 165
Carrot Apple Ginger Juice 166
White Bean and Cauliflower Dip with Baked Pita Chips 168
Roasted Pumpkin Hummus 170
Spinach and Ricotta Egg Muffin Cups 172
Grilled Cheddar and Pear Panini Sticks 174
Superfood Popcorn 176
Apple Power Pockets 179
Beet-Chocolate-Walnut Cookies 180
Cinnamon and Maple Roasted Pumpkin Seeds 182
Carrot Cake Sandwich Cookies 184
Cranberry Granola Bars 186
Beet Chips 188
Homemade Dried Cranberries on Sunflower Seed Butter Logs 190
Carrot-Apple Cinnamon Sticks 192
Pear Sauce 195
Apple Ring Pancakes 196
Maple Almond Butter 199
Purple Panda Smoothie 200
Honey-Wheat Bread 202
Broccoli-and-Cheese Soft Pretzel Knots 204

Fall

AUTUMN IN NEW ENGLAND IS A SEASON OF BEAUTY AND CHANGE: THE START OF A NEW SCHOOL YEAR, THE TURNING OF THE LEAVES, AND THE FIRST COOL BREEZE THAT BRINGS WITH IT THE DESIRE FOR HEARTIER COOKING. FARMERS' MARKETS FILL WITH JEWEL-colored root vegetables, potted mums, and barrels overflowing with pumpkins and gourds.

Growing up in Michigan, I always knew that fall had arrived when we paid a visit to the old Franklin Cider Mill, which served up just-pressed apple cider and warm, homemade cider donuts. Whenever we visit my parents in the fall, I make sure to take the boys for their annual cider-donut splurge. If fall were a flavor, it would taste like a warm cider donut dipped in a cold glass of apple cider. I still enjoy apple cider, but I was all too excited when Sarah introduced me to her Carrot Apple Ginger Juice (page 166), a new staple of my fall repertoire. As a mother, I appreciate its health benefits (and I love that it's become our own family fall tradition), while my boys simply love the flavor.

Let's not forget the return of the school lunch. It can be a daunting feat trying to pack delicious, wholesome, interesting lunches five days a week. Our snacks make the perfect, packable additions to your school lunch routine. Grilled Cheddar and Pear Panini Sticks (page 174) wrap well in parchment paper and are a fun twist on plain grilled cheese. Apple Power Pockets (page 179) are a sweet shake-up of traditional peanut butter and jelly sandwiches. As for interesting sides, we suggest our Kale Chips with Butternut Squash Seed Oil and Sea Salt (page 162) or Beet Chips (page 188) instead of boring old bagged potato chips. Of course, no lunch box is complete without something sweet. Our Carrot Cake Sandwich Cookies (page 184) and Beet-Chocolate-Walnut Cookies (page 180) will make your kids the object of serious lunch-box envy. We suggest packing enough to share!

Fall is synonymous with harvest time. Seek out local farms offering harvest festivals, pick-your-own events, and canning classes. Kids will love picking out pumpkins for the family to carve together, and many farms offer hayrides and corn mazes as an added draw during the harvest season. Plan a family visit to your local apple orchard and stock up on interesting heirloom varieties. Use your harvest in our apple-centered recipes, including Caramel Apples with Sea Salt (page 156), Baked Apple Chips (page 165), and Apple Ring Pancakes (page 196). If you planted a garden of your own, make the fall harvest a family affair and work together to prepare your garden patch for winter, bring plants indoors, and freeze some of the abundant fall produce.

FAVORITE FALL PRODUCE

APPLES	CARROTS	KALE
ARUGULA	CAULIFLOWER	LIMA BEANS
BEETS	CELERY	PEARS
BOK CHOY	CRANBERRIES	PUMPKINS
BROCCOLI	EDAMAME	RASPBERRIES
BROCCOLI RABE	GINGERROOT	SPINACH
BRUSSELS SPROUTS	GRAPES	
CABBAGE	HONEY	

NF Cranberry-Orange Buttermilk Snacking Cake

/ MAKES 6 MINI BUNDT CAKES /

Cranberries, orange zest, and buttermilk come together in these light, fluffy, flavorful cakes. We love to use mini Bundt pans for baking, as they create adorable-looking individually portioned treats. During the baking process the fresh cranberries become slightly caramelized, which increases their sweetness while still maintaining that zesty tang.

- 2½ CUPS WHOLE WHEAT PASTRY FLOUR
- 1 TABLESPOON BAKING POWDER
- ½ CUP PURE CANE SUGAR
- ½ TEASPOON KOSHER SALT
- 2 LARGE EGGS
- 1½ CUPS BUTTERMILK
- 4 TABLESPOONS (¼ CUP) UNSALTED BUTTER, MELTED AND COOLED
- GRATED ZEST OF 2 ORANGES
- 1 CUP CRANBERRIES, SLICED IN HALF
- 3 TABLESPOONS TURBINADO OR OTHER COARSE RAW SUGAR
- WHIPPED CREAM, TO SERVE

1. Position the rack in the top third of the oven and preheat to 400°F. Grease and flour six mini Bundt pans and place on top of a baking sheet.
2. Whisk together the flour, baking powder, cane sugar, and salt in a large bowl.
3. In a small bowl, whisk together the eggs and buttermilk. Whisk in the butter and orange zest. Add the buttermilk mixture to the flour mixture and stir gently to combine. Gently fold in the cranberries.
4. Divide the batter evenly among the prepared pans, smoothing the tops with a spatula, then sprinkle with the turbinado sugar. Bake for 20 to 25 minutes, until a toothpick inserted in the center comes out clean. (It never hurts to test it a few minutes early to avoid a dry cake.) Let the cakes cool in their pans for 10 minutes, then remove and serve warm or at room temperature with fresh whipped cream. Snacking cakes will keep sealed in an airtight container or wrapped tightly in parchment paper or beeswax wrap on the countertop for 3 days. They taste best reheated in a low oven or sliced and toasted.

Cranberries are loaded with antioxidant and anti-inflammatory nutrients that support the immune system and aid in cancer prevention.

Babies of all ages will love the sweet taste and soft texture of this cake. Older infants can hold a piece, while smaller babies can enjoy crumbs.

GF NF Caramel Apples with Sea Salt

/ MAKES 4 SNACKS /

Our family always takes an early fall trip to the nearby orchard for apple picking. We fill our baskets with our favorite heirloom varieties: Jonagold, Northern Spy, Rhode Island Greening, and Cox's Orange Pippin. Although we're all fans of grabbing a plain apple for a snack, every so often it's fun to elevate our daily fruit with a coating of caramel and sprinkle of sea salt for an extraspecial seasonal snack. The stress of making homemade caramel is eliminated from this recipe by melting down high-quality caramel candy. Burning sugar and endless stirring, be gone!

8 OUNCES HIGH-QUALITY CARAMEL CANDIES
SCANT ¼ CUP WATER
4 SMALL APPLES
4 WOODEN SKEWERS
2 TABLESPOONS SEA SALT

1. Put the caramel candies and water into a small saucepan over medium-low heat. Let the candy melt slowly, stirring occasionally. This will take about 10 minutes. It is helpful to use a whisk at the end to break the last pieces down.
2. While the caramel is melting, line a baking sheet with parchment paper and firmly stick the wooden skewers into the apples. When the caramel is ready, slowly dip each apple into the sauce and rotate to coat. Lift the apple up and continue to rotate it above the pot so that the apple catches any excess drips while the caramel is setting up. Place the caramel apple on the prepared baking sheet and sprinkle with some of the sea salt. Repeat with all the apples. Refrigerate the baking sheet of apples for 1 hour to fully set. Caramel apples with sea salt are best enjoyed the day of making, but extra apples can be wrapped tightly in parchment paper and stored on the countertop to enjoy the next day.

Apples offer a healthy dose of fiber, which not only keeps little bellies full but also ensures their digestion system is moving smoothly.

For babies, peel a raw apple and discard the skin, then use your fruit peeler to peel the flesh into small thin ribbons. Slice ribbons into small bites for younger infants to enjoy.

FIELD TRIP

/ HARVEST TIME ON THE FARM /

For many farms, fall is the busiest time of year, with pumpkin patches overflowing, apple trees bending under the weight of their fruit, hayrides, corn mazes, and more. Many small orchards offer a wide range of tasty heirloom-apple varieties for picking, along with a tempting array of apple products including cider, apple butter, and applesauce. Take the whole family along for a fall farm adventure, and while you're there stocking up on apples and carving pumpkins, also keep an eye out for the smaller, sweeter "sugar pumpkins" used in baking. Be sure to pick up a few sugar pumpkins for puree and seeds so you can make our Roasted Pumpkin Hummus (page 170) and Cinnamon and Maple Roasted Pumpkin Seeds (page 182).

Orchard Fresh Fruit

GF NF Brussels Sprout Crisps with Parmesan and Lemon

/ MAKES 2 CUPS /

Brussels sprouts are a vegetable that elicits strong reactions—people either love them or hate them with a passion. However, we're convinced that even many of those who fall in the latter camp will embrace this vegetable when served roasted with a tang of lemon, a pinch of salt and pepper, and a sprinkling of freshly grated Parmesan cheese. The result is crunchy, cheesy, and crispy perfection. Preparing the sprouts can be a bit tedious, so we suggest turning on some fun music!

- 10 OUNCES BRUSSELS SPROUTS
- 2 TABLESPOONS EXTRA VIRGIN OLIVE OIL
- BIG PINCH OF KOSHER SALT
- 5 GRINDS OF BLACK PEPPER
- 1 LEMON, SLICED INTO WEDGES
- 3 TABLESPOONS FRESHLY GRATED PARMESAN CHEESE

1. Preheat the oven to 425°F.
2. Trim off the bottom of each sprout, slice the sprout in half, and using the tip of your knife, cut away the small triangular stem. Peel apart the individual leaves and place them on a baking sheet.
3. Drizzle the olive oil over the leaves, sprinkle with salt and pepper, and toss. Roast for 10 to 12 minutes, until half of the leaves look dark and charred. To serve, dish out portions and top with a squeeze of lemon juice and a sprinkle of the Parmesan cheese. Do this right before eating, as the juice and cheese will wilt the leaves if allowed to sit. These are best served warm from the oven.

Brussels sprouts offer a powerful and unique mix of nutrients that naturally detoxify the body.

Older infants can feed themselves crisp Brussels sprouts chips, while younger babies may want the chips sliced into smaller pieces. If the finishing squirt of lemon juice is too acidic to please baby's palate, simply omit it.

GF NF DF Kale Chips with Butternut Squash Seed Oil and Sea Salt

/ MAKES 2 CUPS /

I have yet to meet a kid who doesn't like kale chips—they are salty, crunchy, and completely addictive. I suggest quietly placing a bowl next to your kids while they're reading or watching a movie. They will quickly plow through the bowl and ask for more without even realizing they're eating their daily greens. While traditional kale chip recipes call for olive oil, we've given things a twist by using butternut squash seed oil, which is made by roasting and pressing the seeds of the squash. Squash seed oils have high amounts of vitamins A and E and carotenoids relative to other commonly used vegetable oils such as canola, grapeseed, and olive oil. It's worth adding this oil option to your pantry, but feel free to substitute another oil in this recipe.

1 BUNCH OF KALE

1 TABLESPOON BUTTERNUT SQUASH SEED OIL

½ TEASPOON SEA SALT

1. Preheat the oven to 225°F.
2. Rip the kale leaves from the stem and tear into bite-size pieces. Rinse and pat dry using a kitchen towel. Toss the dry kale leaves with the oil and salt in a large bowl. With your hands, rub the oil mixture into the leaves so they are fully coated. Spread the leaves in an even layer on a baking sheet and bake for 1 hour. Store kale chips in an airtight bag or container in the pantry. Enjoy within 1 week.

Kale is an excellent source of iron, a mineral that helps transport oxygen to various parts of the body, aids cell growth, and encourages proper liver function. Kale is also a great source of fiber, which is important to the digestive process.

Older infants can grab and munch on a salty kale chip, while younger babies may prefer theirs crumbled into rice or scrambled eggs.

GF NF DF Baked Apple Chips

/ MAKES 2 CUPS /

Slightly crispy, slightly chewy, and very sweet, apple chips are a staple in fall lunch boxes. They are the perfect addition to oatmeal or yogurt. I also like to add these to our Jewel Mix (page 227) instead of, or in addition to, store-bought dried fruits. Packed in an airtight lidded glass container, these will keep in the refrigerator for up to 2 weeks.

1 TABLESPOON CANOLA OIL
4 APPLES
JUICE OF 1 LEMON

1. Preheat the oven to 200°F. Brush a wire rack with canola oil and place it on a baking sheet.
2. Core the apples and cut them into ¼-inch slices. Toss the apple slices in a medium bowl with the lemon juice (to prevent discoloration). Arrange the apple slices on the wire rack and bake for 2 hours. Allow the apple chips to cool completely, then store in an airtight container in the refrigerator.

Apples are a good source of immune-boosting vitamin C, and their high fiber content makes them a filling snack choice.

Older babies will happily chew on an apple chip, while smaller infants will need the chips cut into thin pieces.

GF NF DF Carrot Apple Ginger Juice

/ MAKES 2 SMALL GLASSES /

Back to school often means exposure to a whole plethora of germs. Fall is the perfect time to focus on foods rich in disease-fighting beta-carotene such as carrots, immune-boosting all-stars such as apples, and healing, soothing foods such as ginger. When Sarah feels a cold coming on or one of her boys complains of a stuffy nose, this juice is her first line of defense. She has even served it warm as a soothing, healing beverage.

4 TO 6 CARROTS, PEELED AND ENDS TRIMMED
2 APPLES, CORED AND CUT INTO QUARTERS
ONE 2-INCH PIECE OF FRESH GINGERROOT, PEELED

1. Following the manufacturer's instructions for your juicer, juice the carrots, apples, and ginger together. Pour into 2 glasses and enjoy. Fresh juice can be refrigerated in airtight containers for 1 to 2 days. Gently shake before opening, as freshly packed juice tends to settle.

Ginger relieves many gastrointestinal ailments by relaxing the intestinal tract.

Experiment with your baby's likes and try serving this juice through a straw, spoon-fed, or stirred into brown rice. If the ginger is too strong, simply adjust the mix to satisfy baby's tastes.

love
mom ♡

NF DF White Bean and Cauliflower Dip with Baked Pita Chips

/ MAKES 2 CUPS OF DIP /

White beans and roasted cauliflower pair perfectly in this savory, creamy dip. Garlic and lemon juice plus a pinch of salt and pepper are the only flavorings necessary—the beans and cauliflower pack enough flavor on their own. Homemade pita chips are simple and utterly addicting, especially when served warm from the oven. Present the dip with a basket of warm pita chips and a plate of crunchy fall veggies. This is an easy-to-pack, make-ahead addition to school lunches—just put cooled pita chips into a reusable snack bag, and scoop the dip into a lidded glass container.

FOR THE DIP

1 CUP CAULIFLOWER FLORETS, CUT INTO 1-INCH PIECES
⅓ CUP PLUS 2 TABLESPOONS EXTRA VIRGIN OLIVE OIL
ONE 15-OUNCE CAN CANNELLINI BEANS, DRAINED AND RINSED
1 GARLIC CLOVE
2 TABLESPOONS FRESHLY SQUEEZED LEMON JUICE
½ TEASPOON KOSHER SALT
5 GRINDS OF BLACK PEPPER
¼ CUP CHOPPED FRESH PARSLEY

1. To make the dip, preheat the oven to 425°F. Toss the cauliflower with 2 tablespoons of the olive oil and roast on a baking sheet until tender, about 25 minutes. Turn the oven down to 400°F.
2. Process the roasted cauliflower in the bowl of a food processor with the beans, garlic, lemon juice, salt, and pepper until smooth. With the motor on, stream in the remaining ⅓ cup of olive oil. Turn the motor off, stir in the parsley, and adjust seasonings to taste.
3. To make the pita chips, cut each pita into eight wedges. Arrange the pita wedges on a large baking sheet and brush the top with the olive oil. Sprinkle the wedges with the oregano, a pinch of salt, and the cumin. Bake for 8 to 12 minutes, until light brown.

FOR THE PITA CHIPS

6 PITAS

¼ CUP EXTRA VIRGIN OLIVE OIL

1 TEASPOON DRIED OREGANO

PINCH OF KOSHER SALT

PINCH OF GROUND CUMIN

Cauliflower has a high fiber content, making this cruciferous vegetable a great choice for digestive system support.

The creamy consistency of this dip is perfect for baby. Older infants may enjoy the crunch of a pita chip, but younger babies can have dip on soft bread or a spoon.

GF NF Roasted Pumpkin Hummus

/ MAKES 3 CUPS /

My boys eat hummus by the spoonful, and while plain hummus is always a healthy snack option, it can be nice to mix things up. Pumpkins are a fall food that offers a whole host of health benefits, not to mention deep flavor. And I can't help but love the rich, orange hue of this hummus. We recommend roasting and pureeing an entire pumpkin even though the recipe calls for only one cup of pureed pumpkin. (You can roast the pumpkin up to 3 days ahead of time for this hummus.) Remaining puree can be stirred into maple-syrup-sweetened yogurt, used in baked goods and soups, or simply set aside for baby.

¼ CUP EXTRA VIRGIN OLIVE OIL
1 SMALL SUGAR PUMPKIN
½ TEASPOON KOSHER SALT
6 GRINDS OF BLACK PEPPER
1 SMALL GARLIC CLOVE
TWO 15-OUNCE CANS CHICKPEAS, RINSED AND DRAINED
½ CUP PLAIN WHOLE-MILK OR 2% GREEK YOGURT
2 TEASPOONS ORANGE JUICE
PINCH OF GROUND CUMIN

1. Preheat the oven to 375°F and rub a baking sheet with 2 tablespoons of the olive oil.
2. Cut the stem off the pumpkin and slice it in half around the middle. Using an ice cream scoop, remove the seeds and membranes and discard. Sprinkle the pumpkin flesh with ¼ teaspoon of the salt and 3 grinds of pepper. Place the pumpkin halves, skin side up, on the oiled baking sheet and roast for about 1 hour, until the pumpkin is soft and caramelized around the edges.
3. Scoop out the cooked pumpkin flesh into the bowl of a food processor and discard the skin. Process until smooth. Transfer the pumpkin puree to a bowl and set aside.

4. Into the bowl of the food processor, put the remaining 2 tablespoons of olive oil and the garlic, chickpeas, yogurt, orange juice, cumin, and the remaining ¼ teaspoon of salt and 3 grinds of pepper and process until smooth. Add 1 cup of the reserved pumpkin puree and pulse to just combine. Add more salt and pepper to taste.
5. Serve Roasted Pumpkin Hummus with crisp vegetables, pita chips, or whole grain bread. Pumpkin hummus keeps for 4 days refrigerated in an airtight container.

Sugar pumpkin provides a powerful dose of vitamin A, which supports overall vision and eye health.

Pumpkin hummus has a soft texture and creamy consistency perfect for infants. Babies can enjoy hummus spread on soft bread or spoon-fed.

GF NF Spinach and Ricotta Egg Muffin Cups

/ MAKES 8 STANDARD MUFFINS OR 20 MINI MUFFINS /

Cheesy, rich, and flecked with sautéed onions, garlic, and chopped spinach, these egg cups are perfect for the morning rush. I like to bake these in mini-muffin tins for bite-size snacking, but large muffin tins can be used for breakfast-size portions. The combination of ricotta, mozzarella, and Parmesan cheeses adds a depth of flavor and richness to the recipe. While best served warm, they do pack well in a lidded glass container for a little lunch-box variety. The protein boost provided by the eggs will help kids to feel full and avoid the after-lunch slump.

2 TABLESPOONS EXTRA VIRGIN OLIVE OIL
1 SMALL YELLOW ONION, CHOPPED FINELY
1 GARLIC CLOVE, MINCED
2 EGGS
1 CUP WHOLE-MILK RICOTTA CHEESE
¾ CUP GRATED WHOLE-MILK MOZZARELLA CHEESE
¼ CUP FRESHLY GRATED PARMESAN CHEESE
8 OUNCES SPINACH, CHOPPED (ABOUT 2 CUPS)
PINCH OF KOSHER SALT

1. Preheat the oven to 350°F and grease the muffin tins well.
2. Heat the olive oil in a small skillet over medium heat and sauté the onion until soft, about 5 minutes. Add the garlic and cook for 1 minute more, then remove from the heat.
3. In a medium bowl, whisk the eggs, then add the cheeses and stir. Add the spinach, salt, and the onion mixture and stir.
4. Fill the muffin tins a little more than halfway with batter. Bake standard-size cups for 15 to 20 minutes and bake mini cups for slightly less time, until the tops are golden.

Egg yolks have been given a bad rap for years, but they are one of the richest dietary sources of the B vitamin choline, which is associated with anti-inflammatory properties, as well as increased neurological function. Egg whites offer a low-calorie, low-fat source of protein.

A Spinach and Ricotta Egg Muffin Cup is an ideal protein- and vegetable-packed snack for baby. Older infants can feed themselves a mini cup, while younger babies will enjoy the snack crumbled as finger food.

Grilled Cheddar and Pear Panini Sticks

/ MAKES 9 STICKS /

Sarah's family loves experimenting with grilled-cheese add-ins. There are a million ways to get creative with this sandwich staple, but here is one you might not have considered. Golden, slightly melty pears are the perfect complement to tangy high-quality cheddar. The gooey factor is high in this rich, satisfying sandwich, and when cut into sticks and wrapped in parchment paper, it makes for the perfect on-the-go, easy-to-eat snack.

- 6 SLICES WHOLE GRAIN SANDWICH BREAD
- 2 TABLESPOONS UNSALTED BUTTER, AT ROOM TEMPERATURE
- 1 TABLESPOON HONEY
- 1 CUP SHREDDED OR THINLY SLICED CHEDDAR CHEESE
- 2 PEARS, SLICED THIN
- KOSHER SALT AND GROUND BLACK PEPPER

1. Heat a grill pan or griddle over medium heat. To assemble the sandwiches, butter one side of all the bread slices and lay them, butter side down, on a baking sheet. Spread one-third of the honey onto each of 3 slices and top with ⅓ cup of the cheese. Arrange pear slices on the remaining 3 slices and sprinkle with salt and pepper. Match the sandwich halves together and press to secure.
2. Place the sandwiches onto the hot grill pan and press with a panini press or heavy pot while they toast. Grill for about 3 minutes, until golden and crispy, then remove the press, carefully flip, and grill for another few minutes with the press on. Transfer the sandwiches to a cutting board and slice each one into 3 sticks for snacking.

Pears are a natural source of vitamins C and K and the nutrient copper, all of which act as antioxidants to protect cells from damage.

Doctors consider pears to be a hypoallergenic fruit because they trigger little to no allergic response in most people. Because of this, pears are generally considered "safe" and are often one of the first fruits given to infants. Younger infants can simply snack on soft pear cubes, slices of cheese, and squishy bread while older babies can enjoy an assembled panini stick.

GF NF DF Superfood Popcorn

/ MAKES 6 CUPS /

Did you know that popcorn is a health superstar? It's packed with healthy antioxidants called polyphenols and lots of fiber, but the trick to keeping it healthy is preparing it yourself. Microwave popcorn usually contains unhealthy fats, loads of salt, and unnecessary additives. Keep things simple by popping your own, and up the health benefits by topping with nutritional yeast and spirulina. Just be aware that spirulina can be contaminated with heavy metals such as mercury, so it is very important, especially for children and pregnant women, to eat spirulina from a trusted, high-quality source.

- ¾ CUP NUTRITIONAL YEAST
- ¼ CUP SPIRULINA
- 2 TABLESPOONS KOSHER SALT
- 3 TABLESPOONS CANOLA OIL OR EXTRA VIRGIN COCONUT OIL
- ¾ CUP ORGANIC POPCORN KERNELS

1. To make the superfood topping, simply whisk together the nutritional yeast, spirulina, and salt in a small bowl and carefully pour into a shaker.
2. To make the popcorn, heat the oil in a large pot with a lid over medium-high heat. Pour in the corn kernels, cover, and shake every few minutes. Once the kernels start to pop, shake every minute and continue cooking until the popping slows down. You'll know the popcorn is ready when the popping sound stops.
3. Pour the hot popcorn into a big bowl and liberally sprinkle with the topping. Toss well. Let the seasoned popcorn come to room temperature before eating—we've found that is when it tastes the best.

Spirulina, a blue-green algae, destroys a range of bacteria and infections in the body while strengthening the immune system.

Crisp popcorn can be too hard for small infants to manage, so experiment by shaking the superfood mixture over brown rice or scrambled eggs, or mix it into a favorite spread such as mashed avocado or hummus.

NF DF Apple Power Pockets

/ MAKES 6 MINI POCKETS /

Apples and peanut butter are one of those perfect snacking combinations. These power pockets are a play on the traditional combination, subbing protein-rich almond butter for peanut butter and increasing the apple goodness with a healthy scoop of apple butter. Wrap pita pockets in parchment paper or place in a reusable snack bag, and pop into the lunch box. If you want to avoid brown apples, you can always give the slices a quick toss in lemon juice.

3 MINI WHOLE WHEAT PITA POCKETS
3 TABLESPOONS APPLE BUTTER
3 TABLESPOONS ALMOND BUTTER (OR SUNFLOWER SEED BUTTER FOR A NUT-FREE OPTION)
1 LARGE APPLE, SLICED THIN

1. Warm the pita pockets in the oven or toaster. Slice each pita in half and arrange in a line on the countertop for assembly. Spread ½ tablespoon of the apple butter and ½ tablespoon of the almond butter on the inside of each pocket half, then fill all the pockets with apple slices and enjoy.

Almond butter offers an important dose of protein to build strong muscles and vitamin E to improve skin and hair health.

For older infants who enjoy nuts, create a baby-friendly pocket by peeling the apple flesh with a vegetable peeler to form very thin ribbons, as slices can be hard to chew. If your baby has yet to experiment with nuts, simply omit the almond butter, replace with sunflower seed butter, or serve a simple snack of pita slices and apple ribbons.

Beet-Chocolate-Walnut Cookies

/ MAKES ABOUT 16 COOKIES /

You would never guess these rich, chocolaty cookies are hiding a root vegetable. This is not a case of trying to sneak in vegetables—Sarah and I believe in showing kids what they are eating. Beets just naturally lend sweetness and moisture to baking. Including beets makes for a more flavorful and nutritious cookie.

- 2 MEDIUM BEETS, PEELED AND TRIMMED
- ¾ CUP PURE CANE SUGAR
- ½ CUP PACKED DARK BROWN SUGAR
- 1 STICK (½ CUP) UNSALTED BUTTER, AT ROOM TEMPERATURE
- ½ CUP EXTRA VIRGIN COCONUT OIL, MELTED AND COOLED
- 1 EGG
- 1 TEASPOON PURE VANILLA EXTRACT
- ¼ CUP BUTTERMILK
- 1 TABLESPOON APPLE CIDER VINEGAR
- 2¼ CUPS UNBLEACHED ALL-PURPOSE FLOUR

1. Preheat the oven to 350°F and line 2 baking sheets with parchment paper.
2. Cook the beets in a pot of boiling water until tender, about 15 minutes. Carefully process the beets in a food processor until smooth (you should have about 1 cup of beet puree).
3. In a large bowl, using an electric mixer, beat the cane sugar, brown sugar, and butter until fluffy. Stream in the melted coconut oil and beat for another minute, then add the egg and beat to combine. Add the beet puree, vanilla, buttermilk, and vinegar and stir to combine.
4. In a medium bowl, stir together the flour, cocoa powder, salt, and baking soda. Fold the flour mixture into the wet mixture and stir to combine. Fold in the walnuts and chocolate chips.
5. Use a small ice cream scoop or a spoon to drop evenly spaced dollops of batter (about 2 tablespoons each) onto the prepared baking sheets. Bake for 10 to 15 minutes, until cookies are set, then let the cookies cool for some time on the sheets and transfer them to wire racks to cool completely. Cookies will keep sealed in an airtight container or wrapped tightly in parchment

½ CUP UNSWEETENED COCOA POWDER

½ TEASPOON KOSHER SALT

1 TEASPOON BAKING SODA

¾ CUP CHOPPED WALNUTS

¾ CUP DARK CHOCOLATE CHIPS

paper on the countertop for 3 days. To freeze dough, roll prepared dough into a 2-inch-diameter log, wrap in plastic, and set in the freezer. When ready to bake, slice cookie rounds from the log using a serrated knife.

Beets contain folic acid, which is necessary for the production and maintenance of new cells.

For babies comfortable with walnuts and cocoa, these sweet cookies will make a nutritious treat. Simply omit walnuts for a nut-free cookie. Beet-Chocolate-Walnut Cookies can be eaten whole or crumbled into finger food.

GF NF Cinnamon and Maple Roasted Pumpkin Seeds

/ MAKES 1½ CUPS /

Nothing says fall like the glowing faces of jack-o'-lanterns lighting up the neighborhood. As you scoop out your pumpkin for carving, make sure to save the seeds. With a wide variety of nutrients ranging from heart-healthy magnesium and immune-boosting zinc to healthy fats and muscle-building protein, pumpkin seeds are nutritional powerhouses wrapped up in perfectly tiny, portable packages. Baked with a bit of maple syrup and cinnamon, the seeds become sweet, crunchy, and entirely addictive. Use them to top oatmeal, salads, and soups, or simply grab them by the handful and enjoy!

- 2 TABLESPOONS UNSALTED BUTTER, MELTED
- 2 TABLESPOONS PURE MAPLE SYRUP
- 1 TEASPOON GROUND CINNAMON
- ½ TEASPOON KOSHER SALT
- 1½ CUPS FRESH PUMPKIN SEEDS, CLEANED AND DRIED OFF

1. Preheat the oven to 300°F.
2. In a medium bowl, whisk together the butter, maple syrup, cinnamon, and salt. Add pumpkin seeds and toss until evenly coated.
3. Spread the seeds in a single layer on a baking sheet. Bake for about 40 minutes, stirring occasionally, until golden brown. Watch the seeds very closely during the last 10 minutes to avoid burning. Roasted pumpkin seeds will keep for 3 days stored on the countertop in an airtight container.

Pumpkin seeds contain L-tryptophan, an amino acid that helps with good sleep and lowers depression. Pumpkins also help to give skin a clear, healthy glow thanks to their B vitamins, many minerals (including zinc), phytonutrients, and fatty oils.

Whiz seeds in a food processor or blender to create a fine meal for sprinkling over baby's favorite snacks, including yogurt and applesauce.

Carrot Cake Sandwich Cookies

/ MAKES ABOUT 16 INDIVIDUAL COOKIES OR 8 SANDWICH COOKIES /

The Martha's Vineyard Agricultural Fair comes to the island once a year. Sarah's family counts the minutes until the gates open on this celebration of the island's rich agricultural roots. Her family loves the good old-fashioned fun of Ferris wheels, sheep-shearing competitions, and the blue-ribbon bake-off. Sarah and her son Dylan first entered the children's baking contest with these cookies made using local carrots and Island honey. Moist and light, thanks to the grated carrots, and studded with chopped walnuts and raisins, these cookies mimic the taste of carrot cake. Of course the blue ribbon only confirmed that these cookies are a winner!

FOR THE COOKIES

- 1 CUP UNBLEACHED ALL-PURPOSE FLOUR
- 1 TEASPOON GROUND CINNAMON
- ½ TEASPOON BAKING SODA
- ½ TEASPOON KOSHER SALT
- 1 STICK (½ CUP) UNSALTED BUTTER, SOFTENED
- ⅔ CUP DARK BROWN SUGAR
- 2 TABLESPOONS PURE MAPLE SYRUP
- 1 EGG
- ½ TEASPOON PURE VANILLA EXTRACT

1. To make the cookies, arrange the oven racks in the upper and lower thirds of the oven and preheat the oven to 375°F. Line 2 baking sheets with parchment paper.
2. In a medium bowl, whisk together the flour, cinnamon, baking soda, and salt. In a large bowl, using an electric mixer, beat the butter, sugar, maple syrup, egg, and vanilla until fluffy, about 2 minutes. With a wooden spoon, stir in the carrots, walnuts, and raisins. Add the flour mixture to the wet mixture and stir until just combined.
3. Use a small ice cream scoop or a spoon to drop dollops of batter (about 1½ tablespoons each) about 2 inches apart on the prepared baking sheets. Bake, switching the position of the sheets halfway through, until cookies are set, 10 to 15 minutes. Let the cookies cool on the baking sheets for 10 minutes, then transfer them to wire racks to cool completely, 30 minutes more.

1 CUP COARSELY GRATED CARROTS, ABOUT 2 MEDIUM
1 CUP CHOPPED WALNUTS
½ CUP RAISINS

FOR THE FILLING

8 OUNCES CREAM CHEESE, AT ROOM TEMPERATURE
¼ CUP HONEY

4. While the cookies bake, make the filling: in a small bowl, beat the cream cheese and honey with an electric mixer until smooth.
5. Sandwich 2 cooled cookies together with a heaping tablespoon of cream cheese filling in between.

Walnuts are a rich source of omega-3 fatty acids, monounsaturated fats, and vitamin E, offering antioxidant and anti-inflammatory health benefits.

These soft, sweet, nutritious cookies are a special snack for baby. For infants who have yet to enjoy nuts, simply omit the walnuts. Babies can nibble on a whole cookie or enjoy picking up bite-size crumbs. If you have yet to introduce honey, put aside a few cookies to serve without frosting.

Cranberry Granola Bars

/ MAKES ABOUT 12 BARS /

No snack book would be complete without a killer recipe for granola bars. It is no wonder that grocery-store shelves are overflowing with versions of this packable snack—unfortunately, those are often filled with unhealthy additives and preservatives, as well as loads of sugar. Often, store-bought granola bars are no healthier than a candy bar. However, when you make your own, you can choose wholesome ingredients such as oatmeal, pecans, coconut, wheat germ, dates, and cranberries for a nutritionally balanced, naturally sweet treat. Wrapped in wax paper, these make an easy-to-grab after-school snack or perfect lunch-box treat.

- 2 CUPS OLD-FASHIONED OATMEAL
- 1 CUP CHOPPED RAW PECANS
- 1 CUP LOOSELY PACKED UNSWEETENED SHREDDED COCONUT
- ¼ CUP WHEAT GERM
- 3 TABLESPOONS UNSALTED BUTTER
- ⅔ CUP HONEY
- ¼ CUP DATE OR COCONUT SUGAR
- 1½ TEASPOONS PURE VANILLA EXTRACT
- ¼ TEASPOON KOSHER SALT
- ½ CUP CHOPPED PITTED DATES
- 1 CUP DRIED CRANBERRIES

1. Preheat the oven to 350°F. Line an 8 × 12-inch baking dish with parchment paper and grease the paper.
2. In a medium bowl, stir together the oatmeal, pecans, coconut, and wheat germ. Turn the mixture out onto a separate baking sheet and bake for 10 to 12 minutes, stirring occasionally, until golden and fragrant. Transfer the oatmeal mixture to a large bowl. Reduce the oven temperature to 300°F.
3. In a small saucepan, bring the butter, honey, date sugar, vanilla, and salt to a boil over medium heat. Stir the boiling mixture for 1 minute, then pour it over the oatmeal mixture. Add the dates and cranberries and stir to fully combine.
4. Scoop the mixture onto the prepared baking sheet. With damp fingers, gently press the mixture into the pan. Bake for 25 to 30 minutes, until light brown. Let the cooked bars cool for 3 hours in the baking sheet, then cut into bars.

Coconut improves the body's absorption of calcium and magnesium, helping to build strong teeth and bones.

Older infants who comfortably eat nuts and honey and who have most of their teeth will enjoy snacking on these granola bars either whole or crumbled into small bites. Younger babies can sample from a tray of finely chopped dates and dried cranberries.

GF NF DF Beet Chips

/ MAKES 2 CUPS /

For some reason potatoes, in all their starchy glory, are the most popular vegetable for chips, which is a shame because there are so many healthier options. Take beets for example: with their deep red and gold colors and slightly sweet flavor, these root vegetables become crunchy and crispy when sliced thin and lightly fried in heart-healthy canola oil, rivaling the best potato chip. With a sprinkle of kosher salt, they perfectly walk the line between sweet and savory.

1 CUP CANOLA OIL
2 MEDIUM BEETS
KOSHER SALT

1. To prepare for frying, pour the canola oil into a medium-size saucepan and heat over medium heat. Next, line a baking sheet with an absorbent kitchen towel.
2. While the oil heats up, peel the beets and slice into 1/32-inch slices with a mandoline or sharp knife. Place 1 beet round into the warming oil. When the edges of the round begin to sizzle and fry, the oil is at the ideal cooking temperature.
3. Working in batches, carefully place 6 to 8 rounds into the hot oil (overcrowding the pan will reduce the oil's heat and make soggy chips). Cook the chips for 1½ minutes, flipping halfway through. When the beet slices are crisp and browned, use a slotted spoon to remove the chips to the towel-lined baking sheet; immediately sprinkle with salt and let cool. Repeat the frying process until all the rounds are cooked. Chips are best enjoyed within 2 days and can be stored in a bag in the pantry.

Beets are a good source of phytonutrients that provide antioxidant, anti-inflammatory, and detoxification support.

For an easy baby snack, finely dice a peeled beet and simply steam or sauté the cubes in olive oil until tender.

GF NF DF Homemade Dried Cranberries on Sunflower Seed Butter Logs

/ MAKES 4 SNACKS PLUS EXTRA DRIED BERRIES /

"Ants on a log" is a classic snack. We've added a healthy twist by substituting sunflower seed butter for peanut butter (which is helpful if your child attends a peanut-free school) and homemade dried cranberries for the raisins. If you intend to snack on any leftover cranberries by themselves, you might want to toss them with 2 tablespoons of sugar before baking, as they can be quite sour on their own. Although they aren't as good, you can always substitute ½ cup store-bought dried cranberries for the homemade ones. But just watch the sugar content, as store-bought dried fruit often contains quite a bit of added sugar.

4 CUPS FRESH CRANBERRIES

4 CELERY STALKS

½ CUP SUNFLOWER SEED BUTTER

1. Preheat the oven to 200°F. Line a baking sheet with parchment paper and top with a mesh cooling rack or a finely woven wire rack.
2. Bring a large pot of water to a boil. To blanch the cranberries, pour them into the boiling water and cook until the skins pop and the berries are all split open, about 1 minute. Drain the berries and pat dry with a kitchen towel, making sure to remove all the surface water.
3. Spread the cranberries in a single layer on the rack. Dehydrate the berries in the oven for 4 to 5 hours. When the berries have reached a texture you like, remove them from the oven and let them cool completely.

❹ To assemble the logs, simply spread 2 tablespoons of the sunflower seed butter on each stalk of celery and top with homemade dried cranberries. Slice the logs into thirds and enjoy immediately. Store extra dried cranberries in a glass jar or other airtight container in the pantry for up to 2 weeks for future snacking and baking projects.

Sunflower seed butter is a nutritious source of nonanimal protein, helping to build muscle and provide energy for growing bodies.

Babies will enjoy sunflower seed butter spread on soft bread with thin slices of dried cranberries. Celery tends to be too stringy and crisp for infants.

GF DF Carrot-Apple Cinnamon Sticks

/ MAKES 20 TO 24 STICKS /

Shredded carrots and apples provide the base for these sweet, chewy snacks. The warm flavors come from a combination of cinnamon, ginger, and honey, while oats and pecans add a bit of crunch. These snacking sticks can easily be made gluten free by using your favorite gluten-free flour in place of the whole wheat flour and using rolled oats that have been designated gluten free.

- 1 CUP RAW PECANS
- 1 CUP ROLLED OATS (GLUTEN-FREE IF YOU WISH)
- 1 CUP RAISINS
- ½ CUP WHOLE WHEAT PASTRY FLOUR (OR GLUTEN-FREE FLOUR IF YOU WISH)
- 1¼ TEASPOON BAKING POWDER
- 1¼ TEASPOON GROUND CINNAMON
- ½ TEASPOON GROUND GINGER
- ½ TEASPOON KOSHER SALT
- 2 MEDIUM CARROTS, PEELED AND GRATED
- 1 APPLE, PEELED AND GRATED
- 1 VERY RIPE BANANA, PEELED AND MASHED
- ¼ CUP ORANGE JUICE
- 3 TABLESPOONS HONEY

1. Preheat the oven to 350°F and line 2 baking sheets with parchment paper.
2. Put the pecans, oats, and raisins into the bowl of a food processor and pulse until the mixture resembles coarse sand. Transfer the mixture to a bowl and stir in the flour, baking powder, cinnamon, ginger, and salt. Add the carrots, apple, banana, orange juice, and honey and use your hands to fully combine.
3. Flour your work surface. With well-floured hands, pinch off tablespoon-size portions of dough and gently roll into 2-inch-long sticks. The dough will be quite soft, so you may want to roll them only into rough sticks on the work surface and then finish shaping them right on the baking sheets. Arrange the sticks 1 inch apart on the prepared baking sheets. Bake until the tops and bottoms are lightly browned, 15 to 20 minutes.

Carrots, a rich source of beta-carotene, are excellent for supporting strong vision.

Carrot-Apple Cinnamon Sticks are a perfect teething snack for baby, as they are easy to grasp, soft in texture, and pleasingly sweet.

GF NF DF Pear Sauce

/ MAKES ABOUT 2 CUPS /

Applesauce is a favorite dish at our house, but every now and then it's good to shake things up. Because of pears' natural sweetness, no extra sugar or sweetener is needed. Pick your favorite variety of pear—I love Bartlett and D'Anjou, but any type will work—and warm things up with a cinnamon stick and a splash of vanilla. Our favorite way to enjoy this sauce is straight up or as an accompaniment to pancakes or oatmeal.

8 PEARS
2 TEASPOONS FRESHLY SQUEEZED LEMON JUICE
½ CUP WATER
1 CINNAMON STICK
1 TEASPOON PURE VANILLA EXTRACT

1. Peel the pears and them cut into chunks. Stir together the pears, lemon juice, water, cinnamon stick, and vanilla in a saucepan. Bring to a boil over high heat, then immediately reduce the heat to low and simmer for about 20 minutes, until pears have become soft.
2. Remove the cinnamon stick and puree in the pan using an immersion blender (or transfer to a blender or food processor) to create the consistency that you prefer (slightly chunky or smooth). Pear sauce should be stored in an airtight container in the refrigerator and enjoyed within 1 week.

Pears offer a very good source of dietary fiber, which helps prevent type 2 diabetes and heart disease. Pears are also a powerful food for fighting constipation.

The soft, smooth texture of pear sauce makes it an ideal food for babies. Pears are often one of the first fruits given to infants, as doctors consider pears to be a hypoallergenic fruit, meaning they trigger little to no allergic response in most people. Pears are also very easy to digest.

NF Apple Ring Pancakes

/ MAKES ABOUT 20 RINGS /

These apple rounds are as addictive as donuts, but minus the absurd amount of sugar. The apples become warm, sweet, and melty as the pancake cooks, which eliminates the need for syrup. A great on-the-go breakfast or midmorning treat, these pancakes will be gone the minute the last one leaves the pan.

- 1 CUP UNBLEACHED ALL-PURPOSE FLOUR
- 1 TEASPOON BAKING POWDER
- ½ TEASPOON BAKING SODA
- ¼ TEASPOON KOSHER SALT
- 1 TABLESPOON PURE CANE SUGAR
- 1 TEASPOON GROUND CINNAMON
- 1 EGG, LIGHTLY BEATEN
- 1½ CUPS BUTTERMILK
- 3 TABLESPOONS UNSALTED BUTTER, MELTED, PLUS MORE FOR THE GRIDDLE
- 1 TEASPOON PURE VANILLA EXTRACT
- 4 APPLES

1. Preheat a griddle over medium heat. If serving a crowd, put a baking sheet into the oven and preheat to 200°F.
2. Stir together the flour, baking powder, baking soda, salt, sugar, and cinnamon in a medium bowl. Add the egg, buttermilk, melted butter, and vanilla and whisk. The batter should have small to medium lumps.
3. Peel and core the apples and slice them into ¼-inch-thick rounds.
4. With a pastry brush, brush some butter onto the hot griddle. Using your fingers, dip each apple ring into the pancake batter, turning it to coat evenly. Let excess batter drip into the bowl, then carefully place the battered ring onto the griddle. Repeat until there is no more room on the griddle. Cook the rings for about 3 minutes, until golden brown, then flip and cook the second side for about 3 minutes more. Transfer the cooked pancakes to the baking sheet in the oven to keep them warm until serving, or transfer them to a wire rack to cool for eating

later. Cook the remaining rings in batches, brushing more butter onto the griddle as needed. Eat immediately or let cool completely before storing as snacks. Extra pancakes can be stored in the refrigerator for up to 3 days and reheated in a low oven or toaster oven.

We've all heard the old proverb "An apple a day keeps the doctor away." This couldn't be more true, given apples' rich supply of antioxidants, flavonoids, vitamin C, and dietary fiber, all of which help reduce the risk of diabetes, heart disease, and cancer.

Older babies will enjoy holding and snacking on a whole Apple Ring Pancake, while smaller infants can enjoy bite-size pieces.

GF DF Maple Almond Butter

/ MAKES 1 CUP /

Store-bought nut butter often has large amounts of added sugar, which is entirely unnecessary. Instead, a touch of maple syrup adds natural sweetness and warmth to this almond butter. It's great in smoothies, spread on toast or muffins, and as a dipping sauce for apples, carrots, or celery sticks.

2 CUPS WHOLE RAW ALMONDS, TOASTED
1 TEASPOON CANOLA OIL
1 TEASPOON KOSHER SALT
3 TABLESPOONS PURE MAPLE SYRUP

1. Process the almonds and oil in a food processor for 8 to 10 minutes, until smooth and creamy. Stop the motor every 2 minutes and scrape down the sides to ensure even mixing. Transfer the almond butter into a bowl and stir in the salt and maple syrup.
2. Maple almond butter can be stored in a glass jar in the refrigerator for up to 5 days. Stir before spreading.

Almonds are an excellent source of monounsaturated fat, a healthy fat that has been shown to promote heart health.

Maple almond butter is a creamy spread perfect for babies who are comfortable with almonds. Try it on soft bread or mixed into applesauce, smoothies, oatmeal, or yogurt.

GF DF Purple Panda Smoothie

/ MAKES 2 SMALL GLASSES /

The start of school is filled with emotions for both parents and children. As mothers we worry about everything, including whether our kids are eating a healthy and filling breakfast. Sarah packs this smoothie as an on-the-go breakfast to ensure her boys are properly fueled. Almond butter and almond milk offer a dose of protein, which is important for maintaining energy and feeling full, while blueberries and banana are a natural source of sugar, which provides a fast-acting energy boost. The fruitiness of blueberries and the creaminess of banana and almond butter help to disguise the taste of the spinach, but the health benefits of this superfood, including a hefty dose of fiber, calcium, and protein, are still there.

1 BANANA
½ CUP BLUEBERRIES, FRESH OR FROZEN
1 CUP ALMOND MILK
2 TABLESPOONS ALMOND BUTTER
1 HEAPING CUP PACKED BABY SPINACH

1. Simply blend all the ingredients in a blender until smooth. Pour into 2 glasses and enjoy.

Spinach is one of the most nutrient-dense foods in existence. It is an excellent source of more than twenty different nutrients, including dietary fiber, calcium, and protein, which support the body in a variety of ways, from cancer prevention to cardiovascular health.

Smoothies are an easy way to give your baby a boost of nutrition. If your infant is comfortable with almonds, go ahead and feed this smoothie through a straw, in a sippy cup, or with a spoon. If your child avoids nuts, replace the almond butter and milk with sunflower seed butter and an alternative milk.

NF Honey-Wheat Bread

/ MAKES 2 LOAVES /

Sometimes simple is best, and nothing beats the classic snack of homemade bread with fresh butter. Throw a loaf into the oven right before your kids come home from school and your kitchen will smell warm and comforting when they walk through the door. Honey adds just a touch of sweetness, which goes perfectly with sweet or savory spreads and fillings. Pair Honey-Wheat Bread with a touch of almond butter and shredded apple, or grill slices of it with sharp cheddar, spinach, and pesto sandwiched in between.

- 2 CUPS LUKEWARM WATER
- 2 TABLESPOONS PURE CANE SUGAR
- 1 TABLESPOON DRY ACTIVE YEAST
- 2 TABLESPOONS HONEY
- 3 CUPS UNBLEACHED ALL-PURPOSE FLOUR, PLUS MORE FOR KNEADING
- 2½ CUPS WHOLE WHEAT FLOUR
- 2 TABLESPOONS FLAXSEEDS
- 2 TABLESPOONS WHEAT GERM
- 1 TABLESPOON KOSHER SALT

1. First, proof the yeast: Whisk the water and sugar in a large mixing bowl until the sugar has dissolved. Sprinkle in the yeast and whisk until dissolved, then let sit for 10 minutes. You should see a dense creamy layer on the top of the water.
2. To make the dough, whisk the honey into the water mixture, then add the flours, flaxseeds, wheat germ, and salt and stir to combine. Top with pieces of the 2 tablespoons of butter. Using your hands, knead the ingredients for 5 minutes until they form a smooth, elastic ball.
3. For the first rise, butter a large bowl and coat a piece of plastic wrap with a little oil. Put the ball of dough into the bowl and loosely cover the bowl with the plastic wrap, oil side down. Let the dough rise in a warm place for about 1 hour, until it's doubled in size.

2 TABLESPOONS BUTTER, SOFTENED, PLUS MORE FOR GREASING THE BOWL

1 TABLESPOON EXTRA VIRGIN OLIVE OIL, FOR COATING PLASTIC WRAP

4. For the second rise, first butter two 1-pound loaf pans. Punch down the risen dough and knead it in the bowl a few times. Transfer the dough onto a floured surface and cut in half. Knead each hunk of dough a few times, then place the 2 balls into the prepared loaf pans. Let the pans of dough sit, uncovered, for about 1 hour, until the dough has again doubled in size.
5. When approaching the 1 hour mark on the second rise, preheat the oven to 350°F. When your dough has doubled in size, place the pans in the oven and bake for 35 to 40 minutes, until the tops are lightly browned. Let the loaves cool in their pans for 5 minutes, then turn out onto a wire rack to cool completely.
6. Wrapped tightly in parchment paper or beeswax wrap, the loaves can be kept on the countertop for about 4 days.

Flaxseeds offer a generous dose of fiber, which supports a healthy digestive system.

This soft, sweet loaf is perfectly suited to baby. Plain slices of bread are an easy snack, but you can also treat the bread as an empty canvas for nutritious spreads such as avocado, hummus, olive oil, and nut butters.

NF Broccoli-and-Cheese Soft Pretzel Knots

/ MAKES 8 TO 10 PRETZELS /

I fondly remember a grade school friend who always had boxes of soft pretzels in her freezer for after-school snacks. They came with individual baggies of salt, and we used to beg her mom for seconds (more salt this time!) and load our plates with yellow mustard for dipping. That childhood treat can't hold a candle to these homemade Broccoli-and-Cheese Soft Pretzel Knots. Savory, cheesy, and flecked with broccoli, they are deeply warming and filling, perfect for a lunch-box treat or as a post-sports-practice energy booster. These pretzels are so flavorful that no dipping sauce is required.

- 1 PACKET (2¼ TEASPOONS) ACTIVE YEAST
- 1½ CUPS LUKEWARM WATER
- 1 TEASPOON KOSHER SALT
- 1 TABLESPOON PURE CANE SUGAR
- 4 CUPS UNBLEACHED ALL-PURPOSE FLOUR (OR A MIX OF WHOLE WHEAT AND UNBLEACHED ALL-PURPOSE FLOURS), PLUS MORE FOR KNEADING
- 1 CUP BROCCOLI, STEAMED AND MASHED
- 1 CUP GRATED CHEDDAR CHEESE
- 1 LARGE EGG
- COARSE SEA SALT, FOR TOPPING

1. Preheat the oven to 425°F and line a baking sheet with parchment paper.
2. To make the dough, in a large bowl, sprinkle the yeast into the warm water and stir with a spoon until dissolved. Add the salt and sugar and stir, then slowly add the flour, 1 cup at a time, stirring after each addition until incorporated. Next, stir in the broccoli and cheese.
3. Turn the dough out onto a work surface and knead with your hands until the dough comes together, about 5 minutes. Shape the dough into a ball. Pinch off a golf-ball-size piece of dough. Roll the ball between your hands into a rope, then bring the ends of the rope up so the dough forms a U shape. Twist the 2 ends around each other 3 times, then fold the twisted piece toward you. Press the end down to the bottom of the U to form a pretzel knot. Don't worry about getting a perfect shape. Kids are encouraged to form any fun and creative pretzel shapes they like.

4. Arrange the pretzels on the prepared baking sheet. In a small bowl, whisk the egg, then brush the dough knots with egg and generously sprinkle with salt. Bake the pretzels on the middle rack for 10 minutes, then set the oven to broil. Move the baking sheet to the top rack and broil for about 5 minutes, until the tops are brown. Watch closely to avoid burning.
5. Pretzels taste best warm or at room temperature. Pretzels may be stored in an airtight container on the countertop for up to 4 days, and they freeze well.

Broccoli supplies the body with potassium, which helps maintain a healthy nervous system, improve brain function, and promote regular muscle growth.

Soft pretzels are a perfect snack for baby, as they are tender on the gums, easy to hold, and can be adapted to include your favorite seasonal produce. Depending on your baby's age, chop pretzels into bite-size pieces or serve whole.

WINTER RECIPES

Cinnamon and Date Sugar Almonds 210
Eggnog Smoothie 212
Grapefruit Ginger Juice with Pomegranate Ice 214
Maple Brown Rice Pudding 216
Crispy Root Vegetable Patties with Yogurt-Dill Sauce 220
Roasted Acorn Squash Quesadillas on Flour Tortillas 222
Oven-Baked French Fries 224
Jewel Mix 227
Hot Chocolate with Whipped Coconut Cream 228
Vegetable Dumplings 230
Sweet Potato–Quinoa Nori Rolls 232
Crispy Roasted Chickpeas 234
Winter Granola 236
Sesame Seed Candy 238
Sweet Potato–Cornmeal Muffins 240
Oatmeal-Raisin Cookie Dough Balls 242
Yogurt-Dipped Dried Fruit 244
Mini Roasted Broccoli Pizzas 246
Dark-Chocolate-Dipped Coconut Macaroons 248
Cranberry Gingerbread Cookies 250
Carrot Miso Ginger Spread 252
Kale Bread Pudding Bites 254
Butternut Squash Turnovers 256
Mini Sweet Potato Pies 258
Cauliflower Mac-'n'-Cheese Bites 260

Winter

THE FIRST SNOW IS ALWAYS LIKE SOMETHING OUT OF A FAIRY TALE HERE IN NEW ENGLAND; THE PINE TREES WITH THEIR FINE DUSTING, GENTLE FLAKES WHIRLING IN THE WHIPPING WIND, WHITE AS FAR AS THE EYE CAN SEE. MY BOYS TUMBLE OUTSIDE AFTER SPENDING an hour getting bundled from head to toe, only to be found at the door ten minutes later complaining of cold. Yes, winter is all fun and games for about the first week or two, then it can become difficult to keep up the charade. As much as our family loves building snowmen and sledding down our gently sloped yard, the cold months have a way of wearing us down. That's why nourishing, wholesome, warming food becomes all the more important for keeping our energy stores high.

Winter farmers' markets have become increasingly popular, putting to bed the notion of barren winter pantries. You can expect a variety of goodies, from root vegetables and microgreens to broccoli and Brussels sprouts, as well as yogurt, freshly baked bread, and maple syrup. When the temperature drops and the days grow dark, we begin craving hearty, stick-to-your-ribs foods. All of which are a joy to prepare. There is nothing better than cooking in a warm, fragrant kitchen while the snow swirls outside. After a day of sledding, enjoy Crispy Root Vegetable Patties with Yogurt-Dill Sauce (page 220), a delicious and filling snack. Long, cold, snowy days also provide a good excuse to get the kids in the kitchen. Baking a batch of cookies or muffins is an easy way to pass an icy afternoon indoors. Treat your little bakers to a mug of Hot Chocolate with Whipped

Coconut Cream (page 228) while you whip up a batch of Sweet Potato–Cornmeal Muffins (page 240). Or invite friends over for a fireside game night and serve Maple Brown Rice Pudding (page 216), a warming treat.

The winter months include many reasons to celebrate. The holidays call for festive recipes that nourish visiting relatives and friends. We like to enjoy a bowl of Crispy Roasted Chickpeas (page 234) while gift wrapping, and our Sesame Seed Candy (page 238) makes the perfect stocking stuffer when wrapped in wax paper and tied with colorful twine. Set out bowls of Cinnamon and Date Sugar Almonds (page 210) to welcome guests to your holiday dinner party, and end the night with Dark-Chocolate-Dipped Coconut Macaroons (page 248), always a crowd favorite.

Although there is so much to celebrate during the winter months, as parents we know all too well that the season often brings with it colds, coughs, and general ickiness. Luckily, Sarah has us covered with immune-boosting recipes such as Grapefruit Ginger Juice with Pomegranate Ice (page 214) that prevent and soothe the nastiest symptoms and keep everyone's spirits lifted. Our fruit- and vegetable-focused treats will work on building your family's health from the inside out, making the winter months a time for rosy cheeks and energy aplenty.

FAVORITE WINTER PRODUCE

- BEETS
- BROCCOLI
- BRUSSELS SPROUTS
- CABBAGE
- CARROTS
- CAULIFLOWER
- CITRUS
- COLLARDS
- CRANBERRIES
- GARLIC
- HONEY
- KALE
- LEEKS
- MAPLE SYRUP
- MICROGREENS
- MUSHROOMS
- ONIONS
- PARSNIPS
- POTATOES
- SHALLOTS
- SWEET POTATOES
- TURNIPS
- WINTER SQUASH
- WHEAT GRASS

GF DF Cinnamon and Date Sugar Almonds

/ MAKES 3 CUPS /

When I was a child the fair would come to town once a year, and I remember how the sweet scent of roasting cinnamon-and-sugar nuts would waft through the streets. I loved the crinkly paper cones that would come piled high with the warm, sticky, sweet almonds. Our recipe calls for date sugar, which is a healthy sugar to experiment with. Date sugar is made from dates that are dehydrated and then ground fine. That's it! All the nutrients in the dates are still there in the sugar, along with all the fiber. Our Cinnamon and Date Sugar Almonds also make a thoughtful homemade holiday gift: just put some cooled nuts into a lidded glass jar and embellish with festive ribbon.

1 TEASPOON CANOLA OIL

1 EGG WHITE

1½ TEASPOONS PURE VANILLA EXTRACT

3 CUPS WHOLE RAW ALMONDS

1 CUP DATE SUGAR

3 TABLESPOONS GROUND CINNAMON

½ TEASPOON KOSHER SALT

1. Preheat the oven to 350°F. Line a baking sheet with parchment paper and brush with the canola oil.
2. In a large bowl, beat the egg white until slightly frothy, then stir in the vanilla. Add almonds to the egg mixture and toss to coat.
3. In another large bowl, stir together the date sugar, cinnamon, and salt. Pour the almonds into cinnamon-sugar mixture and toss again. Using your fingers, sift through the mixture and capture the nuts, shaking off excess cinnamon and sugar, then spread the coated almonds on the prepared baking sheet. Bake for 10 minutes, stir, then bake for another 15 minutes. Let them cool completely in the pan.

A great source of protein, almonds help to build strong muscles, and they also contain important minerals like copper and manganese.

If your baby safely enjoys nuts, simply whiz some Cinnamon and Date Sugar Almonds in a food processor to create a fine meal, then sprinkle this special topping on oatmeal, yogurt, or fruit.

GF Eggnog Smoothie

/ MAKES 2 GLASSES /

Traditional eggnog uses a whole lot of raw eggs to achieve the proper creamy consistency. I'm not a big fan of things that include raw eggs, and I certainly wouldn't be comfortable giving them to my boys. This smoothie mimics the warm flavors and creaminess of eggnog while relying on safe, healthy ingredients to achieve the desired consistency, such as whole-milk yogurt, bananas, almonds, and dates. The outcome is surprisingly close to the taste of traditional eggnog—if not a bit creamier and sweeter. The combination of warming spices—vanilla, nutmeg, and cinnamon—makes this a perfect wintry treat. For a nut-free option, you can leave out the almonds without compromising the taste.

1 SMALL RIPE BANANA
1 CUP PLAIN WHOLE-MILK YOGURT
¼ CUP WATER
1 TABLESPOON ROUGHLY CHOPPED RAW ALMONDS
1 TEASPOON HONEY OR MAPLE SYRUP
2 DATES, PITTED
¼ TEASPOON PURE VANILLA EXTRACT
PINCH OF GROUND NUTMEG
PINCH OF GROUND CINNAMON

1. Simply blend all the ingredients together in a powerful blender, pour into 2 glasses, and enjoy!

Yogurt contains protein and calcium, which help to build strong teeth and bones.

An Eggnog Smoothie is a perfect snack for babies who enjoy nuts and honey. If your infant has yet to experiment with these foods, simply leave them out for an equally delicious drink.

GF NF DF Grapefruit Ginger Juice with Pomegranate Ice

/ MAKES 4 SMALL GLASSES /

This freshly squeezed juice is an immunity all-star, with vitamin-C-packed grapefruit and warming, healing ginger. Honey has also been shown to have powerful healing qualities, especially for irritated little throats. The addition of pomegranate-infused ice cubes not only adds a bit of beauty to the glass but also kicks up the health factor, thanks to the seeds' high concentrations of antioxidants. This juice will feel like a special pick-me-up for little ones who are under the weather. Although citrus is not native to the Northeast or Midwest, many farmers partner with other growers across the country to share goods. If you can't find a source at your farmers' market, look for domestically grown Florida citrus, often available at grocers. Additionally, many citrus groves offer boxes of their produce available for shipping. Have a box of grapefruit, oranges, and tangerines shipped directly from the farm to your home. It's like receiving a box of sunshine!

SEEDS FROM 1 POMEGRANATE
1 CUP WATER, PLUS MORE FOR ICE
3 TABLESPOONS HONEY
3 TABLESPOONS THIN SLICES OF PEELED FRESH GINGERROOT
JUICE OF 2 LARGE GRAPEFRUITS
JUICE OF 2 LIMES
SELTZER WATER, TO SERVE

1. To make the ice, sprinkle the pomegranate seeds into an empty ice cube tray to evenly distribute and carefully fill the tray with water. Put it into the freezer and allow to freeze solid.
2. Meanwhile, in a small saucepan, bring the water, honey, and gingerroot to a simmer. Let simmer for 5 minutes to create a syrup. Place the pan of syrup directly into the freezer to cool.
3. While the syrup cools, strain the grapefruit and lime juices into a large pitcher to remove any pulp and seeds, and stir. Strain the cooled syrup into the pitcher, removing the ginger slices, and stir again.
4. To serve, place a pomegranate ice cube in each of 4 glasses, pour in the juice mixture, and top with a splash of seltzer.

Grapefruit is an excellent source of vitamin C, a vitamin that supports the immune system and helps reduce cold symptoms.

You may substitute agave for the honey and skip the fizzy seltzer water (using flat water instead) for younger drinkers. This is a tart juice, but your baby may surprise you and be quite interested!

GF NF DF Maple Brown Rice Pudding

/ MAKES 6 TO 8 SNACKS /

The perfect snack for a cozy afternoon spent at home, our Maple Brown Rice Pudding is quick to throw together, but it does take over an hour of oven time, so plan accordingly. As the rice pudding cooks, your home will fill with the warm fragrances of maple, cinnamon, and vanilla, tempting hungry little ones to the table for a heaping bowl. If you like a bit of crunch with your creaminess, garnish the pudding with a sprinkling of toasted coconut or roasted sunflower seeds, sliced almonds, or other chopped nuts.

- 1/3 CUP LONG-GRAIN BROWN RICE
- 3½ CUPS (TWO 14-OUNCE CANS) FULL-FAT COCONUT MILK
- ½ CUP MAPLE SYRUP
- 1 SMALL PINCH OF KOSHER SALT
- ½ TEASPOON GROUND CINNAMON
- 1 TEASPOON PURE VANILLA EXTRACT

1. Heat the oven to 300°F.
2. Put the rice in a food processor and pulse 10 times to break up the grains a bit and scratch their hulls. Be careful not to over-process.
3. In a 2-quart ovenproof pot or Dutch oven, stir together the cracked rice, coconut milk, maple syrup, salt, cinnamon, and vanilla. Bake, uncovered, for 45 minutes, then stir. Bake for 45 minutes more and stir again. You'll see the milk darkening in color and the rice grains beginning to plump up.
4. Cook for another 45 minutes. Now it will be a deeper brown and starting to thicken into pudding. Taste a rice grain to test for doneness, and bake for another 10 minutes if needed. Be mindful that the pudding will firm up as it cools, so take it out of the oven while it is still a bit soupy.

Maple syrup contains minerals such as zinc and manganese, which allow the immune system to operate at an optimal level.

The creaminess and sweet taste of this pudding make it an ideal snack for baby.

FIELD TRIP

/ MAPLE SYRUP HARVEST /

The process of making maple syrup ("maple sugaring") is rather long and involved, but the end product—our favorite sticky, sweet, pancake-topping syrup—makes it all worthwhile. Maple sap is harvested from February through April, when great vats of it are boiled down over the course of many hours. The process begins when maple trees are "tapped" and the slowly dripping sap is caught in buckets (or by a network of tubes connecting the taps to the sugarhouse). The buckets full of sap are emptied and the sap is transported to the sugarhouse, where it is boiled down until it reaches a sticky, thick consistency and concentrated sweetness. If you live in a cold climate, venture out to a local maple syrup farm to watch the maple-sugaring process. While you might not stay from start to finish, you can certainly have a fun afternoon helping to collect the great buckets of sap and witnessing the beginning of the sweet-smelling boiling process. Of course, you'll want to take home a few bottles of syrup so you can try our Maple Brown Rice Pudding (page 216) and Winter Granola (page 236).

80

GF NF Crispy Root Vegetable Patties with Yogurt-Dill Sauce

/ MAKES 9 TO 12 PATTIES /

One of the best ways to tempt kids to eat their root vegetables is to serve them in a warm, crispy patty with a tangy yogurt-dill sauce. The combination of beets, carrots, and parsnip gives these patties a slightly sweet edge on top of the savory flavorings of garlic and salt. Crunchy, satisfying, and quite addictive, our Crispy Root Vegetable Patties also make a great base for a hearty breakfast. Just throw an egg on top!

FOR THE YOGURT-DILL SAUCE

¾ CUP PLAIN WHOLE-MILK GREEK YOGURT

2 TABLESPOONS CHOPPED FRESH DILL

JUICE OF 1 LEMON

1 GARLIC CLOVE, MINCED

½ TEASPOON KOSHER SALT

1. To make yogurt-dill sauce, simply whisk together the yogurt, dill, lemon juice, garlic, and salt in a small bowl. Cover and refrigerate the sauce until snack time, up to 3 days.
2. To make the patties, wash and peel the beets, carrots, and parsnip. Shred the vegetables using a food processor fitted with grating blade, or grate on the large holes of a box grater. Transfer the grated root vegetables to a large bowl, add the garlic and salt, and stir well to combine.
3. In a medium bowl, beat the egg whites until soft peaks form, then add them to the vegetable mixture. Add the full egg to the vegetables and stir. Do not worry if the batter looks runny.

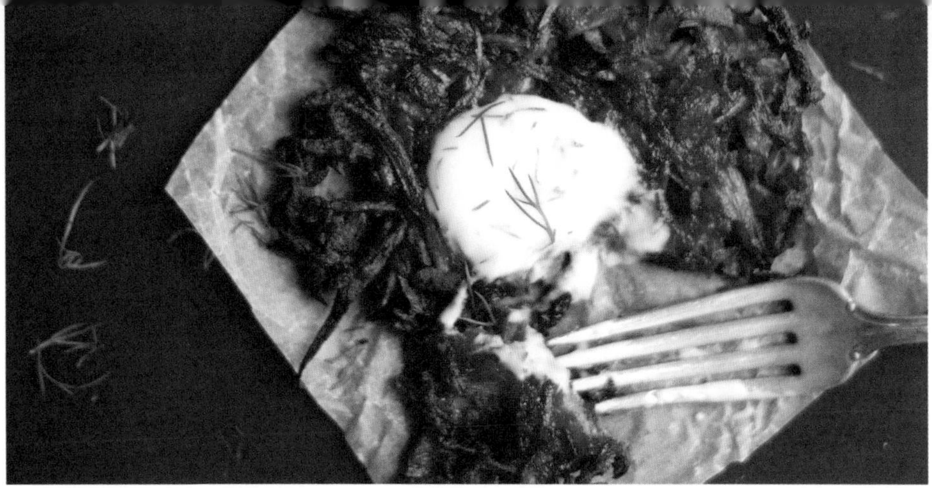

FOR THE PATTIES

2 MEDIUM BEETS

2 MEDIUM CARROTS

1 MEDIUM PARSNIP

2 GARLIC CLOVES, MINCED

½ TEASPOON KOSHER SALT

1 LARGE EGG PLUS 2 EGG WHITES

3 TABLESPOONS CANOLA OIL, FOR PAN FRYING

4. Heat a cast iron skillet over medium heat and coat the bottom with a thin layer of canola oil. Using a ¼ cup measure, scoop up some patty mixture and deposit it onto the skillet, flattening it slightly to form a 3-inch-diameter patty. Repeat until the surface of the pan is full but not crowded. Cook for 5 to 7 minutes, until the undersides are golden brown, then flip the patties and cook for 5 minutes more. The vegetables should be soft all the way through, and the patty should have a crisp crust. Cook the remaining batter in batches, adding more oil as needed. Serve the patties with the yogurt-dill dipping sauce. To store patties, layer them between sheets of parchment paper and place them in an airtight glass container. They will keep in the refrigerator for up to 4 days.

Beets contain tryptophan, also found in chocolate, which relaxes the mind and creates a sense of well-being.

Babies can enjoy small pieces of the vegetable patties with or without a drizzle of sauce. Older infants will enjoy holding a whole patty and self-feeding.

NF Roasted Acorn Squash Quesadillas on Flour Tortillas

/ MAKES 4 TO 6 SNACKS /

Homemade flour tortillas are surprisingly easy to make, and they elevate these quesadillas from ordinary to extraordinary. Roasted acorn squash gets smothered in Monterey jack cheese, topped with black beans, and sandwiched between 2 warm-from-the-oven tortillas. Toasty, melty, and perfect for dipping in salsa, guacamole, or sour cream, quesadillas make a hot-and-hearty after-school snack. You can also pack them for school lunches—just wrap toasted tortillas in aluminum foil, and pack the dipping condiments in separate lidded glass containers. To get a jump on this dish, roast the acorn squash up to 3 days ahead.

1 SMALL ACORN SQUASH
KOSHER SALT
4 FLOUR TORTILLAS (SEE INGREDIENTS BELOW)
ONE 14-OUNCE CAN BLACK BEANS, DRAINED AND RINSED
1 AVOCADO, SLICED
1 CUP MONTEREY JACK CHEESE, SHREDDED

1. Preheat the oven to 375°F and grease a baking sheet.
2. Slice the squash in half around the middle and, using an ice cream scoop, remove the seeds and membranes and discard. Sprinkle the squash flesh with salt. Place the squash, skin side up, on the greased baking sheet and roast until tender and caramelized, about 1 hour. Let the squash cool, then scoop the squash flesh into a small bowl and discard the skin. Mash the squash with a fork.
3. To make the tortillas, stir together the flour and salt in a medium bowl, then add the water and 2 tablespoons of coconut oil and stir to combine. Transfer the dough onto a floured work surface and knead. Add a touch more flour or water, a bit at a time, as needed. Continue kneading until the dough is soft and springy, then let it rest for 5 minutes.
4. Divide the dough into seven balls roughly equal in size. On a floured surface and using a rolling pin, roll them into ¼-inch-thick circles.

FOR THE TORTILLAS

2 CUPS UNBLEACHED ALL-PURPOSE FLOUR

½ TEASPOON KOSHER SALT

¾ CUP WATER

3 TABLESPOONS EXTRA VIRGIN COCONUT OIL, MELTED

5. To cook the tortillas, heat 1 tablespoon of coconut oil in a cast iron skillet and cook each dough circle for roughly 1 minute on each side, until the tortilla is lightly browned. Continue with the remaining dough until all the tortillas have been cooked.

6. To make the quesadillas, put a cast iron skillet or griddle over medium-high heat. Assemble the quesadillas: Put 2 of the tortillas on a work surface. Spread each with half of the mashed squash and pile on half of the black beans, half of the avocado slices, ½ cup cheese and a sprinkle of salt, then top with 2 more tortillas to make 2 quesadilla sandwiches. Place 1 quesadilla on the hot skillet. Grill for a few minutes, flip, and continue to cook until the cheese is melted and fillings are heated through. Cook the other quesadilla. Slice the quesadillas into quarters or sixths and serve immediately with sour cream and salsa. Extra tortillas can be stored wrapped in plastic wrap in the refrigerator for up to 1 week. Tortillas can be stored in the freezer for at least 1 month.

Acorn squash is a good source of vitamin C, an important vitamin for warding off colds and the flu during the cold winter months. Adequate vitamin C intake promotes the health of the immune and skeletal systems.

Older infants can snack on bite-size pieces of quesadilla, while younger infants can practice feeding themselves black beans, avocado slices, and shreds of cheese. The soft roasted squash alone is a perfect spoon-fed food for baby, or it can be mixed with banana or hummus.

GF NF DF Oven-Baked French Fries

/ MAKES 3 TO 5 SNACKS /

I resisted introducing my boys to fried foods for as long as possible, but I can't be held responsible for the actions of my husband! He has a serious weakness for French fries, and from the first taste, my sons were completely in love. Like father, like son, I suppose. Luckily, these oven-baked French fries closely mimic their fried cousins, so my boys don't even know the difference. Don't forget to offer a variety of dipping sauces: ketchup, barbecue sauce, honey-mustard dip, even our Carrot Miso Ginger Spread (page 252). Dipping is half the fun!

3 RUSSET POTATOES
3 TABLESPOONS CANOLA OIL
1 TEASPOON KOSHER SALT
KETCHUP OR DIPPING SAUCE OF YOUR CHOICE, FOR SERVING

1. Slice the potatoes into ¼-inch sticks. Fill a large bowl with water and soak the potato sticks for 30 minutes.
2. Preheat the oven to 450°F. Drain the potatoes, dry them well with a kitchen towel, and toss on a baking sheet with the oil and ½ teaspoon of the salt. Spread the potatoes evenly on the baking sheet and roast for 25 minutes, flip them over, and bake for another 5 minutes, or until golden and crisp. Take the fries out of the oven and sprinkle the fries with the remaining ½ teaspoon of salt. Using a spatula, transfer the fries to plates and enjoy with your favorite dipping sauce.

The skin and flesh of potatoes contain phytochemicals and vitamins that actively protect against cardiovascular disease, respiratory problems, and certain cancers.

Oven-Baked French Fries are easily chopped into small pieces for self-feeding or mashed with the back of a fork for a spoon-fed snack. Older infants will enjoy clutching a fry and feeding it to themselves.

GF DF Jewel Mix

/ MAKES 3 CUPS /

If I were to be completely honest, I would admit that Jewel Mix is hands down the most frequently requested snack in our house. (And lucky for me it is also the easiest to make!) I always have several glass snack containers of this mix on hand for throwing into lunch boxes, sports bags, and my purse. I even keep a few containers in the glove compartment of my car for emergency snack situations! It is always satisfying and offers a bit of sweet, a bit of crunch, and a bit of protein. Keep in mind that this is more of an idea than a recipe, so get your own favorite unsweetened dried fruit, high-quality dark chocolate, and raw nuts (walnuts, cashews, almonds, and so on)—even seeds (sunflower and pumpkin)—and toss them together to make a personalized mix.

1 CUP UNSWEETENED DRIED CHERRIES
½ CUP DARK CHOCOLATE CHIPS (AT LEAST 60% CACAO)
½ CUP GOLDEN RAISINS
1 CUP CHOPPED WALNUTS

1. Simply toss together all the ingredients in a large bowl and divide into snack-size containers for an easy grab-and-go treat.

Dried cherries are a great source of fiber, helping to keep the digestive tract moving.

Babies can enjoy a tray of sliced dried cherries and golden raisins, but the nuts and chocolate bites can be difficult for babies to chew and should be avoided.

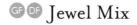

GF DF Hot Chocolate with Whipped Coconut Cream

/ MAKES 4 CUPS /

Real honest-to-goodness hot chocolate is the best part of winter. If that feels like a bold statement, so be it. After a long day on the ski slopes or cheering on your budding hockey player in the freezing stands, I bet everyone will be in agreement. Warming and wonderfully chocolaty, our recipe has the added twist of homemade almond milk and coconut cream for a nutty, rich flavor, but of course cow's milk can be substituted if you prefer.

⅓ CUP UNSWEETENED COCOA POWDER

¼ CUP AGAVE NECTAR

PINCH OF KOSHER SALT

⅓ CUP BOILING WATER

3½ CUPS ALMOND MILK (SEE RECIPE BELOW)

1 TEASPOON PURE VANILLA EXTRACT

½ CUP COCONUT CREAM (CANNED)

FOR THE ALMOND MILK

1 CUP WHOLE RAW ALMONDS

4 CUPS WATER

½ TEASPOON PURE VANILLA EXTRACT (OR MORE FOR A STRONG VANILLA FLAVOR)

CHEESECLOTH FOR STRAINING

1. To make the almond milk, first bring 1 cup of the water to a boil. Measure the almonds into a blender and add the boiling water. Let stand for 30 minutes. Add the remaining 3 cups of water and the vanilla and blend until frothy. Strain the mixture through cheesecloth placed over a jar and discard the solids. Almond milk can be stored in the refrigerator for up to 5 days. Shake before using.
2. To make the hot chocolate, put the cocoa powder, agave, and salt into a saucepan. Whisk in the boiling water. Bring this mixture to an easy boil while you stir. Simmer, continuing to stir, for 2 minutes. Watch that it doesn't scorch. Stir in the almond milk and heat until very hot, but do not boil. Remove the cocoa mixture from the heat and add the vanilla and coconut cream.

FOR THE WHIPPED CREAM

REMAINING COCONUT CREAM, ABOUT 1 CUP (CANNED)

2 TABLESPOONS AGAVE NECTAR

1 TEASPOON PURE VANILLA EXTRACT

3. To make the whipped cream, put the coconut cream, agave, and vanilla into a large bowl and beat with an electric mixer on high speed for 3 to 5 minutes. Whip until the cream becomes fluffy and light with soft peaks.
4. Divide the hot chocolate among 4 mugs and top with whipped coconut cream.

Dark chocolate is a heart- and brain-healthy food, improving blood flow to both vital organs, and it also contains antioxidants that help rid the body of free radicals.

If your baby is enjoying cocoa products, you can offer a few sips of hot chocolate, keeping in mind this is a very sweet treat to be enjoyed in moderation. Babies can also enjoy a spoonful of whipped coconut cream mixed into their oatmeal or atop a smoothie for added creaminess.

NF DF Vegetable Dumplings

/ MAKES 12 DUMPLINGS /

These crispy little pockets of vegetables are bursting with flavor thanks to spicy scallions, fresh ginger, and a pop of sesame oil. Napa cabbage, carrots, mushrooms, and shallot combine into the healthy, hearty filling, which is neatly wrapped in wonton skins and pan fried until golden brown and a bit crispy. A dab of honey helps to sweeten the soy sauce for dipping. Just be sure to look for low-sodium soy sauce, since this condiment is quite salty.

1 SHALLOT
1 CUP SHIITAKE MUSHROOMS
3 TABLESPOONS CANOLA OIL
¾ TABLESPOON MINCED FRESH GINGER
1 CUP FINELY SHREDDED NAPA CABBAGE
1 CUP SHREDDED CARROTS
6 SCALLIONS, SLICED THIN
PINCH OF KOSHER SALT
1 TEASPOON TOASTED SESAME OIL
¼ CUP CHOPPED FRESH CILANTRO
12 WONTON SKINS

FOR THE DIPPING SAUCE

¼ CUP LOW-SODIUM SOY SAUCE
¼ CUP HONEY

1. Put the shallot and mushrooms in the bowl of a food processer and pulse to create a coarse meal. In a medium skillet, heat 1 tablespoon of the canola oil over medium heat. Add the mushroom mixture, ginger, cabbage, carrots, scallions, and the salt and stir to combine. Cook until all the moisture has evaporated, about 6 to 8 minutes. Stir in the sesame oil and cilantro and add more salt to taste. Transfer the filling to a bowl.
2. When ready to assemble the dumplings, line up the bowl of filling, the wonton skins, and a small bowl of water. To assemble each dumpling, place a scant tablespoon of filling in the center of a skin and spread it out a bit with the back of the spoon, leaving some space along the edges. Wet 2 edges of the wonton skin with your finger, and fold the opposite corner over to meet the moistened edges, creating a triangle. Press the seam tightly closed. Repeat until you have made 12 dumplings.

3. To cook, heat a cast iron skillet over medium heat. Add 1 tablespoon of the canola oil, then place six dumplings in the pan. Cook, without flipping, until the wrapper is crisp on one side, about 5 minutes. When the dumplings are nicely browned, add ½ cup of water and place a lid on the pan. Let the dumplings steam until the skins are tender and all the water has evaporated. When the first batch is complete, add the remaining 1 tablespoon of oil and repeat with remaining 6 dumplings.
4. Whisk together the soy sauce and honey to make a simple dipping sauce. Serve with warm or room-temperature dumplings. Dumplings can be stored layered between sheets of parchment paper in an airtight glass container for up to 3 days. To reheat, add dumplings and a splash of water to a covered skillet placed over medium heat.

Cabbage aids in cancer prevention with its antioxidants and anti-inflammatory properties, but steaming or boiling cabbage can strip it of its health benefits, so stick to eating it lightly sautéed or raw.

Older infants can enjoy a chopped dumpling, while younger babies may snack on bites of the filling that have been chopped fine and mixed into brown rice.

GF NF DF Sweet Potato–Quinoa Nori Rolls

/ MAKES 4 SUSHI ROLLS OR 24 PIECES /

While roasting a batch of sweet potatoes for her littlest eater, Gray, Sarah decided to multitask and whip up a few nori rolls for Dylan's lunch box, resulting in this adaptable recipe. Sushi is such a great finger food, with its fresh ingredients tightly swathed in a seaweed wrapper. Perfectly packable—and an exciting twist on traditional school-lunch options—this nori roll includes a trifecta of healthy additions: quinoa, sweet potato, and avocado. We would encourage you to play around with the ingredients to come up with different combinations—think of the roll as a blank canvas. How about the traditional vegetarian combination of brown rice, cucumber, carrots, avocado, and toasted sesame seeds? Or something completely different, such as crumbled hard-boiled egg, asparagus, and spicy mayonnaise? The healthy possibilities are endless.

1 CUP UNCOOKED QUINOA
2 CUPS WATER
2 TABLESPOONS RICE VINEGAR
1 TEASPOON PURE CANE SUGAR
1 SWEET POTATO, PEELED
1 TABLESPOON EXTRA VIRGIN OLIVE OIL
PINCH OF SALT
PINCH OF GROUND BLACK PEPPER
4 SHEETS OF SUSHI NORI (SEAWEED WRAPPERS)
1 AVOCADO, SLICED THIN
LOW-SODIUM SOY SAUCE, FOR DIPPING

1. Preheat the oven to 425°F.
2. In a small saucepan, bring the quinoa and water to a boil, reduce the heat to low, and simmer until the water is fully absorbed, about 15 minutes. Fluff the quinoa with a fork, then stir in the rice vinegar and sugar. Set aside to cool slightly.
3. While the quinoa is cooking, prepare the sweet potato. Slice the sweet potato into ½-inch sticks and toss on a baking sheet with the olive oil, salt, and pepper. Roast for 10 minutes, turn over with a spatula, and cook for about 10 minutes more, until cooked through. Let cool.
4. To roll, place a sheet of nori on your work surface. Spread a thin layer of quinoa over the nori, leaving a 1-inch bare strip at the far edge to seal the sushi. If the quinoa sticks to your fingers, use the back of a spoon. Top the quinoa with a layer of avocado

slices and sweet potato sticks. It doesn't have to be perfect, but try to make it relatively uniform. Wet the far edge of bare nori generously with water. Starting at the end closest to you, roll the nori firmly over the filling and away from you. When the roll is fully closed, press down on it firmly (but not too hard) and set it on your cutting board, seam side down. Repeat with the remaining 3 sheets of nori and fillings. Using a sharp knife, cut each nori roll into 6 equal-ish pieces. Serve with soy sauce for dipping. Nori rolls will keep sealed tightly in an airtight container or wrapped tightly in parchment paper for 3 days. When packing lunch, simply unwrap a roll from the parchment, slice, and place in a sealed container.

Nori is a rich source of protein as well as fiber and omega-3 fatty acids. Nori also contains vitamin C, great for boosting immunity, as well as B2, which is crucial to cognitive function.

Make baby a deconstructed nori roll snack: a pile of quinoa, a scoop of mashed roasted sweet potato, and an avocado slice. You can either mix these ingredients together and spoon-feed them or serve as finger food in little piles.

GF NF DF Crispy Roasted Chickpeas

/ MAKES 1½ CUPS /

Pan roasting chickpeas lends them a nice crispiness, and the combination of cumin, ginger, and turmeric adds a kick of spice. Served warm from the pan these are the perfect snacking food, or they can be added to soups and salads for a hit of flavor and crunch. Experiment with different spice blends depending on your children's tastes.

- ONE 15-OUNCE CAN CHICKPEAS, RINSED AND DRAINED
- 3 TABLESPOONS CANOLA OIL
- 1 TABLESPOON GROUND CUMIN
- 1 TEASPOON GROUND TURMERIC
- ½ TEASPOON GROUND GINGER
- ½ TEASPOON KOSHER SALT
- ¼ OF A FRESH LIME (OPTIONAL)

1. Thoroughly dry the chickpeas on a kitchen towel to remove all residual water (the drier they are the crispier they will be). If chickpea skins become loose or fall off, simply discard them. In a medium bowl whisk together 2 tablespoons of oil, the cumin, turmeric, ginger, and salt. Add the chickpeas and toss to coat.
2. Heat a medium-size skillet over medium-high heat. When the pan is hot, add the chickpeas and gently form into a single layer. Let them cook for 3 minutes without tossing so they begin to crisp up. After 3 minutes add the final tablespoon of oil and toss. Settle the chickpeas back into a single layer and let them crisp up again for another 3 minutes. Toss a final time and leave for 3 minutes longer. Remove them from the hot pan and squeeze fresh lime juice over, then start snacking! Cooled toasted chickpeas can be stored at room temperature in an airtight container for up to 3 days.

Chickpeas supply a high dose of fiber, supporting digestive tract health and helping kids to maintain fullness.

Younger infants will enjoy Crispy Roasted Chickpeas mashed with the back of a fork, while older babies can pop the roasted beans into their mouths for a satisfying snack.

GF DF Winter Granola

/ MAKES ABOUT 4 CUPS /

Our family enjoys granola by the poundful. As soon as I pull a tray full from the oven it mysteriously disappears. While Vijay enjoys his granola sprinkled over oatmeal or simply with milk, Vik loves to eat it by the handful or atop yogurt. I always make a double batch, as it stores well in a sealed glass jar. Homemade granola also makes for a thoughtful holiday gift. Simply allow it to cool, fill a lidded glass vessel, and adorn with ribbon and a sprig of evergreen. This recipe is our favorite, but feel free to experiment with different dried fruits and nuts. Add and subtract accordingly until you have settled on a recipe that will have your family fighting over every last crumb.

1 CUP ROLLED OATS
½ CUP UNSWEETENED SHREDDED COCONUT
½ CUP RAW SUNFLOWER SEEDS
½ CUP RAW HULL-LESS PUMPKIN SEEDS (PEPITAS)
1 CUP SLICED ALMONDS
2 TABLESPOONS CHIA SEEDS
2 TABLESPOONS GROUND FLAXSEEDS
3 TABLESPOONS MAPLE SYRUP
3 TABLESPOONS EXTRA VIRGIN COCONUT OIL, MELTED
½ CUP DRIED, SWEETENED CRANBERRIES

1. Preheat the oven to 350°F.
2. In a large bowl, stir together the rolled oats, coconut, sunflower seeds, pumpkin seeds, almonds, chia seeds, and flaxseeds. Add the maple syrup and coconut oil and stir to coat evenly. Transfer the mixture to a large baking sheet and spread evenly. Bake for 12 to 14 minutes, stirring gently every few minutes. Keep a close eye on the granola toward the end of the cooking time, as it can quickly start to burn.
3. Remove the granola from the oven, give it a toss, and allow it to cool in the pan. Once completely cool, add the dried cranberries and stir well. This granola can be kept at room temperature in a sealed jar for up to 1 week.

Almonds are a source of magnesium and potassium, minerals essential to the health of the nervous system and cardiovascular system.

Older babies who enjoy almonds will be happy to munch on this sweet treat as an easy finger food or atop yogurt. For infants who have yet to try nuts, simply replace the almonds with additional dried fruit or seeds.

NF DF Sesame Seed Candy

/ MAKES ABOUT 20 PIECES /

Chewy, sweet, and studded with crunchy seeds, this peanut-butter-flavored candy is a wonderful holiday treat to bring along to parties or to wrap as a stocking stuffer. Sarah thanks her son's preschool teachers with tins of individually wrapped candies, always making extra for her own sweet-tooth emergencies. The health benefits come from the combination of seeds, as well as the coconut, tahini, and molasses, and you can always swap sunflower seed butter for the peanut butter if a nut-free option is needed.

1 TEASPOON CANOLA OIL
¾ CUP UNSWEETENED SHREDDED COCONUT
1 CUP RAW SESAME SEEDS
½ CUP RAW SUNFLOWER SEEDS
¼ CUP WHEAT GERM
½ CUP TAHINI
¼ CUP PEANUT BUTTER (OR SUNFLOWER SEED BUTTER FOR NUT-FREE VERSION)
¾ CUP MAPLE SYRUP
¼ CUP HONEY
1 TABLESPOON MOLASSES

1. Grease a 9 × 9-inch pan with canola oil.
2. In a medium skillet, stir together the coconut, sesame seeds, sunflower seeds, and wheat germ. Place the skillet over medium heat and toast the coconut mixture, stirring often to prevent burning, until golden, about 5 minutes.
3. In a small bowl, stir together the tahini and peanut butter until smooth. In a small saucepan, heat the maple syrup, honey, and molasses over medium-high heat until boiling. Let the maple syrup mixture boil hard for 5 minutes, then remove from the heat. Add the tahini mixture and stir until combined. Add the toasted coconut mixture and stir well.
4. Spread the candy mixture evenly in the prepared pan and press it down with your fingers. Let the candy cool slightly, then cut it into triangles or bars before it is completely hardened. Let it cool completely, then wrap individual pieces in parchment paper. Enjoy within 4 days.

Coconut helps the body build strong teeth and bones with its calcium and magnesium, while it boosts immunity and helps to ward off infection with its antiviral, antifungal, and antibacterial properties.

As the candy is too brittle and sticky for baby, simply whiz some coconut, sesame seeds, sunflower seeds, and wheat germ in a food processor to form a fine meal, then use this nutritious topping for oatmeal, yogurt, applesauce, or mashed banana.

NF Sweet Potato–Cornmeal Muffins

/ MAKES 10 MUFFINS /

Cornmeal adds heft and a slight crunch to this recipe, and when paired with sweet potato and maple syrup, it renders a muffin that is substantial, filling, and pleasingly sweet. This muffin pairs well with a hearty bowl of chili, and it serves as a sweet, light breakfast when smeared with fruit jam, nut butter, or a drizzle of honey.

- 2 SWEET POTATOES
- 1½ CUPS CORNMEAL
- 1½ CUPS WHOLE WHEAT PASTRY FLOUR
- 2 TEASPOONS BAKING POWDER
- 2 TEASPOONS KOSHER SALT
- ½ CUP HEAVY CREAM
- 1 STICK (½ CUP) BUTTER, MELTED
- ½ CUP MAPLE SYRUP
- 2 EGGS
- 2 TABLESPOONS RAW SUNFLOWER SEEDS

1. Preheat the oven to 375°F and line a 12-cup muffin tin with a total of 10 paper liners.
2. To prepare the sweet potatoes, bring a pot of water topped with a steamer to a boil. Peel the sweet potatoes and chop into 1-inch chunks, steam until fork tender, about 10 minutes. Mash the cooked sweet potatoes in a bowl using a hand masher, or puree in a food processor for a smoother consistency.
3. Stir together the cornmeal, flour, baking powder, and salt in a large bowl. In a medium bowl, stir together 1 cup of mashed sweet potato and the cream, butter, maple syrup, and eggs. Add the sweet potato mixture ingredients to the cornmeal mixture and stir until just combined.
4. Using an ice cream scoop or large spoon, evenly distribute the batter among the prepared muffin cups and sprinkle the top of each muffin with a pinch of sunflower seeds. Bake for 20 to 25 minutes, until a toothpick inserted into the center of a muffin comes out clean. Muffins will keep sealed in an airtight container on the counter for 3 days, and they taste best reheated in a low oven or sliced in half and toasted.

Sweet potatoes, with their orange hue, offer a hearty dose of beta-carotene, which the body converts into vitamin A, important for healthy skin and eyes.

Sweet Potato–Cornmeal Muffins are a baby-friendly snack; simply leave off the sunflower seed topping and crumble muffins into bite-size pieces. For infants just starting solid foods, stick with a simple serving of mashed sweet potato.

GF NF DF Oatmeal-Raisin Cookie Dough Balls

/ MAKES ABOUT 15 BALLS /

Who doesn't love sneaking bites of cookie dough straight from the bowl? My boys even fight over who gets to lick the spoon clean, and I can't blame them. Cookie dough is sometimes better than the actual cookie, which is probably the reason these cookie dough balls are so addictive. Rolled oats give these bites their heft, while dates, raisins, and maple syrup add natural sweetness. Use your favorite cookie as inspiration for experimenting with different add-ins; simply sub chocolate chips for the raisins, or add shredded coconut, nuts, or other dried fruits. This is a great recipe for older children to make from start to finish, as it doesn't require knife skills or involve heat.

1 CUP OLD-FASHIONED OATS (GLUTEN-FREE IF YOU WISH)
1 TABLESPOON EXTRA VIRGIN COCONUT OIL, MELTED
¼ CUP MAPLE SYRUP
½ CUP PITTED DATES
1 TEASPOON PURE VANILLA EXTRACT
1 TEASPOON GROUND CINNAMON
¼ TEASPOON KOSHER SALT
½ CUP RAISINS

1. Put the oats, melted coconut oil, maple syrup, dates, vanilla, cinnamon, and salt into the bowl of a food processor and pulse to just combine. Add the raisins and gently pulse a few times to combine, being careful not to overprocess. Transfer the dough into a medium bowl.
2. Scoop out a heaping tablespoon of dough and roll it between your palms to form a golf-ball-size treat. Place the rolled ball on a clean tray and continue rolling the remaining dough into balls. Cookie dough balls will keep sealed in a tin on the countertop for 3 days.

A true whole grain, oats offer a combination of protein and fiber, keeping bellies full and supporting the digestive system.

Adjust the size of the cookie dough balls based on your child. You can roll very small balls as snacks for younger babies or simply stir a spoonful of the mix into applesauce, mashed sweet potato, mashed banana, or yogurt for additional nutrition.

GF NF Yogurt-Dipped Dried Fruit

/ MAKES 6 SNACKS /

This recipe is incredibly adaptable depending on the preferences of your little ones. You can use any type of dried fruit, and the topping choices are endless. We found that slightly sweetened yogurt pairs well with shredded coconut, slivered almonds, and raw sunflower seeds. However, you might try cinnamon and sugar, finely chopped toasted walnuts, pistachio nuts, chia seeds, even cacao nibs. The dipping and decorating is half the fun, so spread out some wax paper and invite your kids to help you without worrying about the drips and mess.

2 TABLESPOONS MAPLE SYRUP
1 CUP PLAIN WHOLE-MILK YOGURT
½ CUP DRIED PLUMS
½ CUP DRIED APRICOTS
½ CUP DRIED MANGO STRIPS
2 TABLESPOONS UNSWEETENED SHREDDED COCONUT
2 TABLESPOONS SLIVERED ALMONDS (OR YOUR FAVORITE NUT-FREE TOPPING)
2 TABLESPOONS RAW SUNFLOWER SEEDS

1. Line a baking sheet with parchment paper.
2. In a small bowl, stir together the maple syrup and yogurt. Holding one end with your fingertips, dip a dried plum, apricot, or mango strip into the yogurt, coating three-quarters of the piece. Let the excess yogurt drip off, then lay the dipped fruit on the prepared baking sheet and sprinkle it with some of the coconut, almonds, or sunflower seeds. Repeat with the remaining dried fruit pieces. Place the baking sheet in refrigerator and chill until the yogurt sets up, about 30 minutes. Yogurt-Dipped Dried Fruit keeps in an airtight container in the refrigerator for about 3 days.

Dried plums, like most dried fruits, are full of fiber, which prevents constipation and helps the digestive system flow smoothly.

Slice the Yogurt-Dipped Dried Fruit into very small pieces for a baby-friendly snack, or simply cut the dried fruit into fine dice and stir it into your baby's favorite yogurt.

NF Mini Roasted Broccoli Pizzas

/ MAKES 6 PIZZAS /

On wintry Sunday afternoons, Sarah's family gathers in the kitchen to make individual pizzas using her husband's famous pizza-dough recipe. Dylan helps to roll out the dough and sprinkle on the toppings. This healthy and delicious combination of mashed whole tomatoes, mozzarella cheese, and roasted broccoli florets is the family favorite. Don't be scared off by the homemade pizza dough—it is quite easy and doesn't even require kneading. (However, store-bought dough also works just fine.) The dough needs to sit at room temperature for 18 hours, so prepare it the night ahead.

2 BALLS FRESH PIZZA DOUGH (SEE INGREDIENTS BELOW)
1 HEAD OF BROCCOLI, CUT INTO SMALL FLORETS (ABOUT 2 CUPS)
2 TEASPOONS EXTRA VIRGIN OLIVE OIL, PLUS MORE FOR DRIZZLING
1¼ TEASPOONS SALT
ONE 14-OUNCE CAN WHOLE SAN MARZANO TOMATOES
3 TABLESPOONS CORNMEAL
2 CUPS SHREDDED WHOLE-MILK MOZZARELLA CHEESE
PINCH OF GROUND BLACK PEPPER

1. To make the dough, whisk together the flour, salt, and yeast in a medium bowl. Stirring well with a wooden spoon, gradually adding the water. Form the dough into a rough ball using your hands and transfer to a large clean bowl. Cover the bowl with plastic wrap and let the dough rise at room temperature until it has more than doubled in size, about 18 hours.
2. Transfer the dough onto a floured work surface and cut into 4 equal portions. Form 2 portions into balls. (You will need 2 for this recipe; the remaining dough can be tightly wrapped and stored in the refrigerator to use within 3 days or frozen for future baking.) Cover the dough with a damp kitchen towel and let rest on the work surface until soft and pliable, about 1 hour.
3. To make the pizzas, preheat the oven to 425°F. On a baking sheet, toss the broccoli florets with the olive oil and ¼ teaspoon of the salt. Roast until brown, 20 to 25 minutes.
4. Meanwhile, in a small bowl, sprinkle the tomatoes with the re-

FOR THE DOUGH (MAKES 4 BALLS)

4 CUPS UNBLEACHED ALL-PURPOSE FLOUR
2 TEASPOONS KOSHER SALT
¼ TEASPOON ACTIVE DRY YEAST
1¾ CUPS WATER

maining 1 teaspoon of salt and mash them with a fork to break the whole tomatoes into small pieces.

5. On the floured surface, divide each dough ball into thirds. With a wooden rolling pin, roll each ball into a circle approximately 4 inches across. You should have 6 pizza crusts. Sprinkle 2 baking sheets with the cornmeal and place 3 pizza crusts on each baking sheet.

6. Turn the oven up to 450°F. Top each pizza crust with salted tomatoes, cheese, and broccoli. Sprinkle all the pizzas with a pinch of salt and pepper, then drizzle with olive oil. Bake for 10 to 12 minutes, until the cheese is melted and the crusts are crispy.

Overcooking broccoli can render it mushy, tasteless, and drained of nutrients. Roasting broccoli brings out its flavor while maintaining nutrients, which include vitamins K and C and kaempferol, a flavonoid with anti-inflammatory properties that is useful for children with allergies.

Older infants will enjoy pizza cut into small cubes, while younger babies can snack on strands of mozzarella cheese and reserved broccoli.

GF NF Dark-Chocolate-Dipped Coconut Macaroons

/ MAKES 20 COOKIES /

Pillowy puffs of coconut are dipped in rich dark chocolate and rolled in chopped pistachio nuts. Our macaroons are not overly sweet—in fact there is no sweetener in the body of the cookie. The sweetness comes instead from the dark chocolate dip, but a thumbprint of fruit jam would also be quite delightful. If you prefer a plain macaroon, sweeten the batter with a couple tablespoons of agave nectar before baking.

3¾ CUPS UNSWEETENED SHREDDED COCONUT
2 TABLESPOONS COCONUT CREAM
¼ CUP EXTRA VIRGIN COCONUT OIL
1 CUP COCONUT MILK
2 EGGS
½ TEASPOON PURE VANILLA EXTRACT
PINCH OF KOSHER SALT
1 CUP CHOPPED DARK CHOCOLATE
2 TABLESPOONS HEAVY CREAM
½ CUP PISTACHIO NUTS, CHOPPED (OPTIONAL; OMIT FOR NUT-FREE VERSION)
FRUIT JAM (OPTIONAL)

1. Preheat the oven to 350°F and lightly grease a baking sheet.
2. Process 2 cups of the shredded coconut in a food processor for 3 minutes to create a fine meal.
3. In a large bowl, using an electric mixer, beat the coconut cream and coconut oil until well combined and fluffy. (Break apart any large pieces of coconut oil as necessary.) Add the coconut meal, the remaining 1¾ cups of shredded coconut, and the coconut milk, eggs, vanilla, and salt to the whipped oil and cream. Beat to combine.
4. Using a tablespoon measure, spoon small mounds of batter onto the greased baking sheet. Bake for 25 to 30 minutes, until lightly golden. Let cool for 30 minutes.
5. While the macaroons cool, heat the chocolate and heavy cream together—in a microwave oven or by the double-boiler method—and stir to combine. (To use the double-boiler method, put the chocolate and cream into a metal or glass bowl and suspend over a pot of boiling water, stirring to melt the chocolate evenly.) Dip the cooled macaroons in the melted

chocolate and place on a platter. While still warm, sprinkle the dipped macaroon with the chopped nuts and allow to set up.

6. If you prefer a fruit jam topping instead of a chocolate dip, use a teaspoon to press a small well into the center of each warm macaroon and spoon in a little dollop of jam. Macaroons are best enjoyed within 3 days.

Pistachio nuts are a rich source of vitamin B6, which supports blood health and the nervous system.

Older infants can snack on a whole plain macaroon without the chocolate, and younger infants can enjoy nibbling on crumbled pieces. Use dips and toppings that your infant enjoys instead of the chocolate and nuts. Experiment with crumbling a plain macaroon on top of yogurt, oatmeal, or mashed sweet potato.

NF Cranberry Gingerbread Cookies

/ MAKES 3 DOZEN COOKIES /

Nothing brings out holiday cheer like a marathon cookie-baking session. Although at first I was doubtful that anything could replace my traditional gingerbread recipe, I made room in my cookie repertoire for these Cranberry Gingerbread Cookies. I found that the rich, warm gingerbread that I love—which draws its flavor from a combination of cinnamon, ginger, allspice, cloves, and molasses—was enhanced by the presence of sweet, warmed dried cranberries. The cranberries add a jewel-like element to the batter, and the cookies bake into perfect pillowy clouds of warm, spicy sweetness.

3 CUPS UNBLEACHED ALL-PURPOSE FLOUR
1 TEASPOON BAKING SODA
¾ TEASPOON GROUND CINNAMON
¾ TEASPOON GROUND GINGER
½ TEASPOON GROUND ALLSPICE
½ TEASPOON GROUND CLOVES
½ TEASPOON KOSHER SALT
1 STICK (½ CUP) UNSALTED BUTTER, AT ROOM TEMPERATURE
¼ CUP EXTRA VIRGIN COCONUT OIL, MELTED
½ CUP LIGHT BROWN SUGAR
⅔ CUP MOLASSES
1 EGG
1 CUP DRIED CRANBERRIES

1. Preheat the oven to 350°F and position the racks in the top and bottom thirds of the oven.
2. Whisk together the flour, baking soda, cinnamon, ginger, allspice, cloves, and salt in a medium bowl.
3. In a large bowl, using an electric mixer, beat the butter and coconut oil at high speed until well combined. Add the brown sugar and beat until the mixture is light and fluffy, about 2 minutes. Beat in the molasses and egg.
4. Add the flour mixture and cranberries to the wet ingredients and, using a wooden spoon, gently stir to make a stiff dough. Divide the dough in half, then shape each half into a thick disk and wrap in plastic wrap. Refrigerate until well chilled, about 3 hours. (The dough can be kept in the refrigerator for up to 2 days.)
5. To roll out the cookies, work with one disk at a time. Remove a disk of dough from the refrigerator and let stand at room temperature for about 30 minutes. If the dough has been chilled

for longer than 3 hours, it may need even longer to warm to a soft texture that is easy to handle and roll. Place the dough on a lightly floured work surface and sprinkle the top with flour. Roll out the dough to ⅛ inch thick, making sure that it isn't sticking to the work surface. Sprinkle the surface with more flour if needed. If you prefer softer cookies, roll out the dough slightly thicker. Using cookie cutters, cut out the cookies and transfer to ungreased baking sheets, arranging them 1 inch apart.

6. Bake 10 to 12 minutes, until the edges of the cookies are set and crisp. Let the cookies cool on the baking sheets for 2 minutes, then transfer to wire racks to cool completely. The cookies can be stored in airtight containers at room temperature for 1 week.

Molasses is an incredibly rich source of iron, which our bodies need to carry oxygen to our blood cells. It is also a great source of calcium and magnesium, crucial for the strength and development of bones.

Babies, especially those teething, will love to hold and suck on a sweet gingerbread cookie. For younger infants, slice the dried cranberries very thin before adding them to the gingerbread dough, then crumble a baked cookie into manageable bite-size pieces.

GF NF DF Carrot Miso Ginger Spread

/ MAKES 2 CUPS /

This versatile dip can be used as a sandwich spread, tossed with pasta, mixed into brown rice, served alongside an omelet or fried egg, or dolloped onto a veggie stir-fry. It also shines when used as a spread on crackers or a warm slice of crusty bread. The dip's distinct Asian flavor is thanks to the combination of rice vinegar, sesame oil, miso, and freshly grated ginger. In case you are unfamiliar with miso, it is a traditional Japanese fermented seasoning. Fermented foods offer a wealth of health benefits, especially for the digestive tract, thanks to their probiotics, enzymes, vitamins, and minerals. The base that holds all these flavors together—and gives the spread its lovely orange color—is simply finely grated carrots. Because this recipe involves nothing more than measuring and shaking, it's a great place to start for older children who want to prepare something on their own, from start to finish. For a truly gluten-free version, make sure your miso is gluten free.

½ CUP MISO PASTE
¼ CUP PLUS 2 TABLESPOONS CANOLA OIL
1 CUP FINELY GRATED CARROT
2 TABLESPOONS FINELY GRATED GINGER
2 TABLESPOONS RICE VINEGAR
1 TABLESPOON TOASTED SESAME SEEDS
2 TEASPOONS TOASTED SESAME OIL
2 TABLESPOONS HONEY
¼ CUP WATER

1. Put all the ingredients into a sealable container, such as a mason jar, then cover and shake vigorously until well combined. This spread will keep in an airtight container in the refrigerator for 5 days.

Ginger is a powerful digestive aid, helping to soothe gas and relax the intestinal tract.

Depending on your baby's tastes and age, you may reduce or leave out the fresh ginger and substitute honey for maple syrup. Babies may enjoy Carrot Miso Ginger Spread on soft bread, stirred into brown rice, or tossed with scrambled eggs or chickpeas.

NF Kale Bread Pudding Bites

/ MAKES ABOUT 15 BITES /

Sarah's savory bread pudding combines the heartiness of crusty bread with the warm, satisfying flavors of sautéed kale, garlic, and onions and the decadent cheesiness of golden baked Parmesan cheese. An egg and cream custard holds the bread and kale mixture together and gives the dish its firm consistency. This is the perfect breakfast dish on a snowy morning, starting the day out right with a combination of protein, vegetables, and carbohydrates.

- 1 LOAF COUNTRY-STYLE CRUSTY BREAD
- 1 GARLIC CLOVE, MINCED
- ¼ CUP PLUS 1 TABLESPOON EXTRA VIRGIN OLIVE OIL
- 1⅛ TEASPOON KOSHER SALT
- 6 GRINDS OF BLACK PEPPER
- 1 LARGE BUNCH OF LACINATO KALE
- 1 YELLOW ONION, CHOPPED FINE
- 3 CUPS HEAVY CREAM
- 8 EGGS
- ⅓ CUP FRESHLY GRATED PARMESAN CHEESE

1. Preheat the oven to 375°F. Line two 12-cup muffin tins with a total of 15 paper liners.
2. Cut the bread into 1-inch cubes. Put the bread cubes into a large bowl and toss with the garlic and ¼ cup of the oil to coat. Spread the cubes out on large rimmed baking sheet, sprinkle with ⅛ teaspoon of the salt and 3 grinds of the pepper, and bake for about 20 minutes, until golden and slightly crunchy. Transfer the toasted cubes back to the large bowl.
3. Turn the oven down to 350°F. Tear the kale leaves from their stems, then wash the leaves thoroughly and chop into fine ribbons. Discard the stems.
4. Heat the remaining 1 tablespoon of oil in a large skillet over medium-high heat and add the onion and kale ribbons. Sauté until the onions are soft and the juices have evaporated, about 10 minutes.

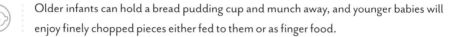

5 Add the kale mixture to the toasted bread cubes and toss. In a separate bowl, whisk together the heavy cream, the eggs, the remaining 1 teaspoon of salt, and the remaining 3 grinds of pepper. Add the egg mixture to the bread mixture, stir, and let sit for 15 minutes.

6 Spoon a heaping ¼ cup of bread pudding into each prepared muffin cup and sprinkle the tops with the cheese. Bake the pudding cups for 25 to 30 minutes, until set and the tops are golden. Let the pudding cups stand for 10 minutes in the tins before snacking.

Kale is high in calcium, which aids in building strong bones and maintaining a healthy metabolism.

Older infants can hold a bread pudding cup and munch away, and younger babies will enjoy finely chopped pieces either fed to them or as finger food.

NF Butternut Squash Turnovers

/ MAKES 8 TURNOVERS /

Butternut squash is such a versatile winter ingredient. It sweetens well for baking, while it adds depth and warmth to savory dishes such as soups and stews. For these turnovers, butternut squash is used as a creamy filling, and orange zest, brown sugar, cinnamon, and nutmeg play up its sweetness factor. If you're scared of using puff pastry (it's so thin and fancy!), this is a great recipe to help you conquer your fear. Simply cut the rolled-out pastry into squares, brush the edges with egg, and heap filling in the middle, then fold to make a triangle and press closed with a fork. No fancy folding techniques needed. The result is a light, flaky handheld pastry oozing with rich, warm, sweet butternut squash.

- 1 POUND BUTTERNUT SQUASH, PEELED AND CUT INTO ½-INCH CUBES
- 2 TABLESPOONS EXTRA VIRGIN OLIVE OIL
- ¼ TEASPOON SALT PLUS A PINCH
- PINCH OF GROUND BLACK PEPPER
- 1 TEASPOON GRATED ORANGE ZEST
- 3 TABLESPOONS ORANGE JUICE
- 3 TABLESPOONS DARK BROWN SUGAR
- 1 TABLESPOON UNBLEACHED ALL-PURPOSE FLOUR

1. Preheat the oven to 425°F and line a baking sheet with parchment paper.
2. Toss the squash cubes with olive oil, a pinch of the salt, and the pepper on a baking sheet. Spread the squash out in an even layer on the baking sheet and roast for about 25 minutes, until soft but not mushy. Let the squash cool slightly, then transfer to a large bowl. Add the orange zest, orange juice, sugar, flour, cinnamon, nutmeg, and the remaining ¼ teaspoon of salt and toss. Mash with a potato masher until well combined.
3. Flour a work surface and, using a rolling pin, lightly roll the sheet of pastry into a 12 × 14-inch square. Cut the sheet into 8 small squares. Brush the edges of each square with the egg and neatly place 2 heaping tablespoons of filling in the center of each square. Fold the pastry diagonally over the squash mixture and seal by pressing the edges with a fork.

¼ TEASPOON GROUND CINNAMON, PLUS MORE FOR SPRINKLING
⅛ TEASPOON GROUND NUTMEG
1 SHEET FROZEN PUFF PASTRY (FROM A PACKAGE OF 2), DEFROSTED
1 EGG, BEATEN

4. Transfer the assembled turnovers to the prepared baking sheet. Brush the tops with egg wash, sprinkle with cinnamon, and make 2 small slits with a knife. Bake for 15 to 20 minutes, until browned and puffed. Serve warm or at room temperature. Butternut Squash Turnovers keep sealed on the countertop for 3 days. Reheat turnovers in a low oven or toaster oven for best results.

Butternut squash provides significant amounts of potassium, important for bone health, and vitamin B6, essential for the proper functioning of the nervous and immune systems.

Babies will enjoy a piece of butternut squash turnover chopped into small bites. For infants who might not handle chewing the puff pastry layers, simply add the butternut squash filling to yogurt or oatmeal for a warm, sweet snack.

NF Mini Sweet Potato Pies

/ MAKES 12 PIES /

Kids love working with dough, so this is a great recipe to get them involved. Let them help with the mixing, rolling, and cutting. For adorable handheld pies, we use a small circular cookie cutter and cut stars from the dough scraps for placing on top of the pies. The result is a festive bite-size treat with a warm filling of sweet potato flavored with maple, cinnamon, and vanilla.

FOR THE CRUST

- 1¼ CUPS UNBLEACHED ALL-PURPOSE FLOUR
- ½ TEASPOON KOSHER SALT
- 1 STICK (½ CUP) COLD UNSALTED BUTTER, CUT INTO SMALL CUBES
- ¼ CUP ICE WATER

FOR THE FILLING

- 1 LARGE SWEET POTATO (ABOUT 1 POUND)
- 1 STICK (½ CUP) BUTTER, MELTED AND COOLED
- ¾ CUP DATE OR COCONUT SUGAR
- ¼ CUP MAPLE SYRUP
- ½ CUP PLUS 1 TABLESPOON HALF-AND-HALF

1. To make the crust, put the flour and salt into a food processor and pulse to combine. Add the butter and pulse until the mixture resembles coarse meal, with just a few pea-size pieces remaining. Stream in the ice water, continuing to pulse, until the dough is crumbly but begins to pull away from the sides of the bowl and form a ball. Do not overprocess. Turn the dough out onto a work surface and form into a ¾-inch-thick disk. Wrap tightly in plastic wrap and refrigerate until firm, at least 1 hour.
2. Preheat the oven to 375°F
3. To make the filling, peel and chop the sweet potato into 1-inch cubes and put into a steaming basket over boiling water. Steam until soft, about 15 minutes. Transfer the sweet potato into the bowl of a food processor and process until smooth. Add the butter, date sugar, maple syrup, ½ cup of the half-and-half, and the eggs, cinnamon, and vanilla. Pulse until the mixture is smooth.
4. To assemble the pies, remove the dough from the refrigerator and let it stand for 5 minutes to soften. Transfer the dough onto a floured work surface, roll into a ¼-inch thick sheet, then using

2 EGGS

½ TEASPOON GROUND CINNAMON

1 TEASPOON PURE VANILLA EXTRACT

a round cookie cutter or the rim of a glass, cut out 12 circles of dough to fit inside a mini muffin tin (a pint glass is the perfect size). Gather up the scraps of dough and form them into a ball, then roll out the dough again and, using a small star-shaped cookie cutter, stamp out decorations for the tops of the pies.

5. Press the circles of dough into the cups of a muffin tin, crimping the edges with a fork. Fill each dough cup with 2 heaping tablespoons of filling and place a dough star on top. Brush the pies with the remaining 1 tablespoon of half-and-half. Bake for about 35 to 40 minutes, until the tops are golden. Carefully remove the pies from the pan and let cool on a wire rack.

Sweet potatoes contain anti-inflammatory nutrients that help support brain and nerve tissues throughout the body.

Younger infants can nibble on crumbles of pie, while older babies can easily hold a pie and munch away.

NF Cauliflower Mac-'n'-Cheese Bites

/ MAKES 20 BITES /

As you can imagine, the Vineyard is a quiet, sleepy place during the winter months, so Sarah's family looks to the great outdoors to keep things lively. Snowy trail hikes, afternoon pond skating, and weekends full of sledding ensure hearty appetites, and nothing is more satisfying in a stick-to-your-ribs kind of way than a steaming, cheesy bowl of this pasta favorite. Sarah prepares small ramekins of the pasta and stores them in the refrigerator so that when the snowy group arrives home, a filling snack is just minutes away. Roasted cauliflower enhances the flavor and creaminess of the cheese sauce while adding a hearty dose of vitamin C and fiber to keep little snow bunnies happy and healthy.

1½ CUPS CAULIFLOWER FLORETS, FINELY CHOPPED
½ YELLOW ONION, FINELY CHOPPED
1 TABLESPOON OLIVE OIL
1 TEASPOON PLUS A SPRINKLE KOSHER SALT
1 POUND BOW-TIE PASTA
ONE 8-OUNCE PACKAGE CREAM CHEESE
1 EGG
1 TEASPOON DIJON MUSTARD
8 GRINDS BLACK PEPPER
2 CUPS GRATED SHARP CHEDDAR CHEESE

1. Preheat the oven to 400°F. Line two 12-cup muffin tins with a total of 20 paper liners, and bring a large pot of water to a boil.
2. Toss the chopped cauliflower and onion with the olive oil. Sprinkle the vegetables with salt and lay them on a baking sheet. Roast in the oven for 15 minutes, or until golden brown.
3. While the vegetables roast, cook the pasta according to the package instructions, draining it 2 minutes before the suggested al dente cooking time and reserving ½ cup of the pasta water.
4. In a large bowl, whisk together the cream cheese and ½ cup of hot pasta water until thoroughly combined. Whisk the egg into the thinned cream cheese, then stir in the salt, mustard, black pepper, cheddar cheese, and roasted vegetables.
5. Add the cooked pasta to the cauliflower cheese sauce and stir well to combine. Spoon a heaping ¼ cup of pasta and cheese mixture into each of the prepared muffin-tin cups. Bake for 15 to 18 minutes or until the tops of the bow ties are golden brown.

Cauliflower is an excellent source of vitamins C and K, which offer antioxidant and anti-inflammatory benefits.

Break apart a baked Cauliflower Mac-'n'-Cheese Bite for younger babies, pulling out the pasta and chopping finely.

Acknowledgments

THE WRITING OF THIS BOOK spanned the course of a year—and a busy year at that. We could never have done it alone, and we have so many friends to thank for their support, especially the Matouk family, Sarah Jagger, Elizabeth Cecil, Asya Palatova of Gleena Ceramics, Kaitlyn Bouchard, the Kenner family, the Gaskill-Rasmussen family, the Thompson family, Elise Swartwood, the Russo-Kleeman family, as well as Tea Lane Farm and the Farm Institute.

A big thank you to our agent, Linda Roghaar, our editor, Jenn Urban-Brown, and the entire Roost family—we are honored to be among your inspiring roster of authors.

To all the farmers and food producers who supplied the lovely ingredients that inspired our recipes, we owe you our deepest gratitude for providing our families with local, fresh, lovingly grown ingredients.

CHRISTINE

First and foremost, my mother has my deepest appreciation. You were far ahead of the trends in teaching me to eat seasonal, fresh, home-cooked food. As a mother I now understand the immense effort it takes to feed a family, and I am, more than ever, humbled by your efforts. And a special thanks to my dad for his constant love and unwavering support.

I could never have built such a beautiful family and life without the love and support of my husband, Vijay. I thank God for you every single day.

A special thanks to Liz Murray. I am forever indebted to you for the love you've shown Vijay and Vik.

A heartfelt thank you to the many readers who have supported my blog from its very humble beginning.

Finally, my deepest love and gratitude go to my boys, Vijay and Vikram, for teaching me, challenging me, and rewarding me daily. Being your mother is my true calling and my greatest joy in life. I hope you'll always know how deeply I love you, my bunnies.

SARAH

First, I would like to thank the hard-working people of Martha's Vineyard for welcoming us into your tight-knit community. We are so thankful to be raising our boys on such a magical island.

A humble thanks to my parents. I live everyday with the goal to create a home full of unconditional love, warmth, and trust like the one you made for us.

To my sister Anna—thank you for being my best friend, confidant, and original cooking partner. To my girlfriends, all inspiring and loving women, thank you for your friendships.

Thank you to my husband, Nick. We fell in love watching Iron Chef and cooking pizza in your Cape Cod kitchen, and years later you built me a kitchen, the heart of our family home. Thank you for choosing me.

Last, thank you to my boys, Dylan and Gray. Every middle-of-the-night feeding, birthday cake, and pot of winter soup has been made with gratitude for you. You are my dreams come true, the loves of my life.

Resources

FARMERS' MARKETS AND PICK-YOUR-OWN FARMS

FARMERS' MARKET ONLINE—farmersmarketonline.com. Structured as an open-air market online, this site offers produce, nuts, grains, and specialty foods from real vendors.

LOCALHARVEST—localharvest.com. Search for farmers' markets and available CSA shares easily by zip code. This site also sells products offered by family farmers, such as seeds, soaps, and preserves.

PickYourOwn.org. A national listing of pick-your-own farms organized by state and region.

USDA NATIONAL FARMERS MARKET DIRECTORY—http://search.ams.usda.gov/farmersmarkets/. The United States Department of Agriculture hosts this searchable database of farmers' markets. The site allows visitors to search by zip code, state, products available, and payment accepted.

GARDENING

FARMERS' ALMANAC—farmersalmanac.com. Knowing when to plant is a key to gardening success. *The Farmers' Almanac,* an old and trusted publication, offers practical data such as the last frost date, and gardening calendars as well as articles, blog posts, and videos to help gardeners hone their green thumb.

KGI GARDEN PLANNER—gardenplanner.kgi.org. My community garden uses this tool to plan our plots for maximum yield. This online planner allows you to tailor results to the size of your garden as well as your growing zone.

KidsGardening.org. The National Gardening Association created this resource to encourage both schools and families to dig in and garden.

CHILDREN'S KITCHEN SUPPLIES

CURIOUS CHEF—curiouschef.com. A wide variety of child-friendly cooking supplies from safe vegetable peelers and pizza cutters to small rolling pins and chef's hats.

KUHN RIKON KINDERKITCHEN SERIES—kuhnrikon.com. Whimsical, child-safe and appropriate-size kitchen knives, measuring spoons and cups, whisks, and stirring spoons.

KITCHEN TOOLS

BREVILLE—breville.com. We highly recommend Breville's juicers. All models offer a heavy-duty motor, are easy to clean, and have large produce feed chutes to cut down on chopping/prep time.

CUISINART—cuisinart.com. A basic Cuisinart food processor is our favorite because it is simple to use, durable, and dishwasher safe. We also use the Cuisinart frozen yogurt, ice cream, and sorbet maker and recommend it because it freezes desserts quickly, offers a large-capacity bowl, and is easy to use.

VITAMIX—vitamix.com. We recommend a Vitamix blender. It is an investment but will last a lifetime and become a kitchen staple. Vitamix blenders are commercial grade with a powerful motor that has the ability to chop, cream, blend, grind, and churn. They are easy to clean, and come with a five-year full warranty.

CLEANING PRODUCTS

DR. BRONNER'S MAGIC SOAPS—drbronner.com. For over 150 years, Dr. Bronner's has been making organic, fair-trade soaps and personal care products.

ECOVER—ecover.com. A line of plant-based household cleaners for fabric care, dish soap, cleaning products, and hand care.

ENVIRONMENTAL WORKING GROUP—ewg.org. An organization of scientists, researchers, and policy makers committed to protecting human health and the environment, their consumer guides to cosmetics, produce, and cleaning products are invaluable resources. Before purchasing any cosmetics or cleaners, I always check EWG's consumer guide to get a complete picture of the ingredients and toxicity of the product in question.

THE HONEST CO.—honest.com. Offering cleaning products, bath and body products, diapers, and baby-care products, the Honest Co. creates eco-friendly, safe, and sustainable products.

Seventh Generation—seventhgeneration.com. Cleaning products and various household products derived from plant-based ingredients. Always opt for unscented versions to avoid unnecessary additives.

TRAVEL AND STORAGE CONTAINERS

Glass Jars and Containers

DURALEX—duralexusa.com. A trusted company out of France, Duralex makes wonderful tempered-glass storage containers with great durability.

MASON JARS—Found at almost any home store, mason jars are molded glass jars used for storing food and canning. We especially like kid-sized mason jars that come with handles and lids (see our Raspberry Lemonade, page 120, for a visual).

WEAN GREEN—weangreen.com. Durable glass storage containers with brightly colored snap-tops are perfect for packing and storing snacks and lunches.

WECK JARS—weckjars.com. Timeless, high-quality glass jars perfect for food storage, drinking, and home canning.

Stainless Steel Containers

LUNCHBOTS—lunchbots.com. A wonderful variety of stainless steel lunch containers are offered by LunchBots. Our favorites include the bento containers as well as the insulated containers, which are leakproof and keep food hot on the go.

MIGHTY NEST—mightynest.com. With a pledge to provide only toxin-free products made out of the safest materials, Mighty Nest is a favorite source for lunch gear, fabric snack bags, kitchen products, reusable bottles, and more.

WILD MINT—wildmintshop.com. Dedicated to providing the best nontoxic and eco-friendly products on the market, Wild Mint is a great source for everything from lunch gear and reusable bottles to kitchen essentials and bath and body products.

Portable Cups

CUPPOW—cuppow.com. Imagine being able to turn any canning jar into a spill-free, easy-to-sip cup. These sipping lids for glass jars eliminate the need for wasteful paper coffee cups.

LIFEFACTORY—lifefactory.com. Innovative, BPA-free glass bottles with colorful silicone sleeves, these are our favorite water bottles, hands-down. There are several useful products available, including water bottles with both flip caps and straws, food storage containers, and baby bottles.

THERMOS—thermos.com. Offering a wide variety of products designed to keep foods hot or cold, Thermos is a trusted brand in on-the-go food storage. Look for their stainless steel products, which we prefer.

OTHER

ABEEGO BEESWAX WRAP—abeego.com. Made by coating cotton or hemp with beeswax, jojoba oil, and tree resin, Abeego's beeswax wraps are sustainable, reusable, and nontoxic. We especially like the Big and Little Pockets for storing sandwiches.

BEESWRAP—beeswrap.com. The beeswax coating makes the fabric waterproof, airtight, flexible, and adhesive enough to behave like plastic wrap. The wraps work well for covering plates, or bowls, as well as wrapping sandwiches, cheese and deli purchases, and loaves of bread.

COCO STRAW—Amazon.com. Stainless steel, easy-to-clean, reusable straws.

ZIPZICLE—Amazon.com. BPA-free, plastic flavored-ice pouches.

Recipes by Category

DRINKS

Blueberry Lassi GF NF 133
Carrot Apple Ginger Juice GF NF DF 166
Eggnog Smoothie GF 212
Grapefruit Ginger Juice with Pomegranate Ice GF NF DF 214
Hot Chocolate with Whipped Coconut Cream GF DF 228
Melon Slushies GF NF DF 106
Pea-Avocado Smoothie GF NF DF 93
Purple Panda Smoothie GF DF 200
Raspberry Lemonade GF NF DF 120

BREAKFASTS

Apple Ring Pancakes NF 196
Berry and Cream Scones with Whipped Honey Butter NF 86
Blueberry Baked Oatmeal Cups GF NF 110
Butternut Squash Turnovers NF 256
Cherry, Coconut, and Walnut Bread 80
Cranberry Granola Bars 186
Green Waffles NF 70
Lemon-Glazed Blueberry Donuts 148
Peach Olive Oil Muffins NF DF 130
Raspberry French Toast Sticks GF NF 60
Raspberry-Lemon Whole Wheat Mini Pancakes NF 134
Ratatouille Baked Egg Cups GF NF 62
Spinach and Ricotta Egg Muffin Cups GF NF 172
Strawberry Rhubarb Crumb Muffins 64

Sweet Potato–Cornmeal Muffins NF 240
Winter Granola GF DF 236
Yogurt-Granola Cups with
Homemade Cherry Sauce GF NF 44
Zucchini Bread with Honey-Apricot
Glaze DF 128

LUNCHES AND SIDES

Apple Power Pockets NF DF 179
Asparagus Fries with Parmesan
Cheese GF NF 43
Baba Ghanoush GF NF DF 138
Baked Apple Chips GF NF DF 165
Beet Chips GF NF DF 188
Black Bean Cakes NF DF 136
Broccoli-and-Cheese Soft
Pretzel Knots NF 204
Brussels Sprout Crisps with
Parmesan and Lemon GF NF 160
Bunny Rabbit Rolls GF NF 116
Carrot-Apple Cinnamon Sticks GF DF 192
Carrot Miso Ginger Spread GF NF DF 252
Cauliflower Mac-'n'-Cheese Bites NF 260
Cherry Tomato Cheddar Bites GF NF 105
Cinnamon and Date Sugar Almonds GF DF 210
Cinnamon and Maple Roasted
Pumpkin Seeds GF NF 182
Creamy Asparagus Dip with
Flax Crackers GF 58
Crispy Roasted Chickpeas GF NF DF 234
Crispy Root Vegetable Patties
with Yogurt-Dill Sauce GF NF 220
Feta-Cucumber Dip GF NF 144
Fresh Summer Roll with
Peanut Dipping Sauce GF DF 140
Grilled Cheddar and Pear
Panini Sticks NF 174
Grilled Corn on the Cob with
Lime Butter GF NF 102
Grilled Green Beans with
Lemony Yogurt Dipping
Sauce GF NF 114
Hard-Boiled Eggs with Kale Pesto GF 76
Homemade Dried Cranberries on
Sunflower Seed Butter Logs GF NF DF 190
Honey-Wheat Bread NF 202
Jewel Mix GF DF 227
Kale Bread Pudding Bites NF 254
Kale Chips with Butternut Squash
Seed Oil and Sea Salt GF NF DF 162
Leek Fritters NF 66
Maple Almond Butter GF DF 199
Mini Roasted Broccoli
Pizzas NF 246
Oven-Baked French Fries GF NF DF 224
Oven-Dried Stone Fruit GF NF DF 124

Pear Sauce GF NF DF 195
Raspberry Guacamole GF NF DF 89
Roasted Acorn Squash Quesadillas on Flour Tortillas NF 222
Roasted Pumpkin Hummus GF NF 170
Roasted Sesame Peas GF NF DF 57
Sugar Snap Peas with Honey-Mustard Dip GF NF 90
Spinach Puff NF 72
Spring Vegetable Spears with Dipping Bar GF NF DF 46
Strawberry Fruit Leather GF NF DF 68
Summer Corn Fritters NF 100
Superfood Popcorn GF NF DF 176
Sweet Potato–Quinoa Nori Rolls GF NF DF 232
Tomato-Scallion Biscuits NF 146
Twice-Baked Mini Red Potatoes GF NF 74
Vegetable Dumplings NF DF 230
White Bean and Cauliflower Dip with Baked Pita Chips NF DF 168
Yellow Cherry Tomato and Fresh Mozzarella Pesto Bites GF 118
Yogurt-Dipped Dried Fruit GF NF 244
Zucchini and Squash Wheels with Marinara Dipping Sauce NF 126

DESSERTS

Beet-Chocolate-Walnut Cookies 180
Caramel Apples with Sea Salt GF NF 156
Carrot Cake Sandwich Cookies 184
Cherry Chocolate Pudding Pops GF NF DF 50
Cherry Coconut Lime Flavored Ice GF NF DF 82
Cranberry Gingerbread Cookies NF 250
Cranberry-Orange Buttermilk Snacking Cake NF 154
Dark-Chocolate-Dipped Coconut Macaroons GF NF 248
Green Smoothie Pops GF NF DF 104
Grilled Nectarine Skewers with Toasted Coconut GF NF DF 142
Heat Wave Pops GF NF DF 123
Honey Frozen Yogurt–Dipped Strawberries GF NF 49
Maple Brown Rice Pudding GF NF DF 216
Mini Sweet Potato Pies NF 258
Oatmeal-Raisin Cookie Dough Balls GF NF DF 242
Peach Frozen Yogurt GF NF 108
Quinoa Pudding with Raspberries and Pecans GF NF 84
Rhubarb-Lemon Biscotti NF 94
Sesame Seed Candy NF DF 238
Strawberry Frozen Yogurt Sandwiches GF NF 52

Index

agave nectar
- Berry and Cream Scones with Whipped Honey Butter, 86
- Blueberry Lassi, 133
- Hot Chocolate with Whipped Coconut Cream, 228–29
- as an ingredient, 30
- Melon Slushies, 106
- Peach Frozen Yogurt, 108
- Quinoa Pudding with Raspberries and Pecans, 84
- Raspberry Lemonade, 120–21
- Raspberry-Lemon Whole Wheat Mini Pancakes, 134
- Strawberry Fruit Leather, 68

almond butter
- Apple Power Pockets, 179
- health benefits, 179
- Maple Almond Butter, 199
- Purple Panda Smoothie, 200–201

almond meal
- as an ingredient, 28, 32
- Lemon-Glazed Blueberry Donuts, 148

almond milk
- homemade, recipe for, 228
- Hot Chocolate with Whipped Coconut Cream, 228–29
- Purple Panda Smoothie, 200–201

almonds
- Cinnamon and Date Sugar Almonds, 210–11
- Eggnog Smoothie, 212–13
- health benefits, 199, 211, 237
- as an ingredient, 32
- Maple Almond Butter, 199
- Winter Granola, 236–37
- Yogurt-Dipped Dried Fruit, 244–45

apples
- Apple Power Pockets, 179
- Apple Ring Pancakes, 196–97
- Baked Apple Chips, 165
- Blueberry Baked Oatmeal Cups, 110–11
- Caramel Apples with Sea Salt, 156–57
- Carrot-Apple Cinnamon Sticks, 192–93
- Carrot Apple Ginger Juice, 166–67
- health benefits, 157, 165, 197

apricots
- health benefits, 129
- Oven-Dried Stone Fruit, 124
- Yogurt-Dipped Dried Fruit, 244
- Zucchini Bread with Honey-Apricot Glaze, 128–29

asparagus
- Asparagus Fries with Parmesan Cheese, 43
- Creamy Asparagus Dip with Flax Crackers, 58–59
- health benefits, 43
- Spring Vegetable Spears with Dipping Bar, 46–47

avocados
- Black Bean Cakes, 136–37
- Fresh Summer Rolls with Peanut Dipping Sauce, 140–41
- health benefits, 89, 141
- Pea-Avocado Smoothie, 93
- Raspberry Guacamole, 89
- Roasted Acorn Squash Quesadillas on Flour Tortillas, 222–23
- Sweet Potato–Quinoa Nori Rolls, 232–33

bananas
- Blueberry Baked Oatmeal Cups, 110–11
- Carrot-Apple Cinnamon Sticks, 192–93
- Eggnog Smoothie, 212–13
- Green Smoothie Pops, 104
- Pea-Avocado Smoothie, 93
- Purple Panda Smoothie, 200–201

basil
- Creamy Asparagus Dip with Flax Crackers, 58–59
- health benefits, 119
- kale pesto, 76–77
- Yellow Cherry Tomato and Fresh Mozzarella Pesto Bites, 118–19

beans, white and black
- Black Bean Cakes, 136–37
- health benefits, 137
- Roasted Acorn Squash Quesadillas on Flour Tortillas, 222–23
- White Bean and Cauliflower Dip with Baked Pita Chips, 168–69

beets
- Beet Chips, 188–89
- Beet-Chocolate-Walnut Cookies, 180–81
- Crispy Root Vegetable Patties with Yogurt-Dill Sauce, 220–21
- health benefits, 181, 189, 221

beverages
- Blueberry Lassi, 133
- Carrot Apple Ginger Juice, 166–67
- Eggnog Smoothie, 212–13
- Grapefruit Ginger Juice with Pomegranate Ice, 214–15
- Hot Chocolate with Whipped Coconut Cream, 228–29
- Melon Slushies, 106
- Pea-Avocado Smoothie, 93
- Purple Panda Smoothie, 200–201
- Raspberry Lemonade, 120–21

blackberries
- health benefits, 123
- Heat Wave Pops, 123

blender, 19

blueberries
- Berry and Cream Scones with Whipped Honey Butter, 86–87

blueberries (*continued*)
Blueberry Baked Oatmeal Cups, 110–11
Blueberry Lassi, 133
health benefits, 87, 133, 149
Heat Wave Pops, 123
Lemon-Glazed Blueberry Donuts, 148–49
Purple Panda Smoothie, 200–201
bread, crackers. *See also* muffins, biscuits, scones
Broccoli-and-Cheese Soft Pretzel Knots, 204–5
Cherry, Coconut, and Walnut Bread, 80–81
flax crackers, 58–59
flour tortillas, 116–17, 222–23
Honey-Wheat Bread, 202–3
Kale Bread Pudding Bites, 254–55
pita chips, 144, 168–69
pizza dough, 246–47
Raspberry French Toast Sticks, 60–61
Raspberry-Lemon Whole Wheat Mini Pancakes, 134–35
Zucchini Bread with Honey-Apricot Glaze, 128–29
broccoli
Broccoli-and-Cheese Soft Pretzel Knots, 204–5
health benefits, 205, 247
Mini Roasted Broccoli Pizzas, 246–47
Brussels sprouts
Brussels Sprout Crisps with Parmesan and Lemon, 160–61
health benefits, 161

cabbage
health benefits, 231
Vegetable Dumplings, 230–31
carrots
Bunny Rabbit Rolls, 116–17
Carrot-Apple Cinnamon Sticks, 192–93
Carrot Apple Ginger Juice, 166–67
Carrot Cake Sandwich Cookies, 184–85
Carrot Miso Ginger Spread, 252–53
Crispy Root Vegetable Patties with Yogurt-Dill Sauce, 220–21
health benefits, 193
Spring Vegetable Spears with Dipping Bar, 46–47
Vegetable Dumplings, 230–31
cashew nuts, as an ingredient, 32
cauliflower
Cauliflower Mac-'n'-Cheese Bites, 260–61
health benefits, 169, 261
White Bean and Cauliflower Dip with Baked Pita Chips, 168–69
cheese
Asparagus Fries with Parmesan Cheese, 43
Broccoli-and-Cheese Soft Pretzel Knots, 204–5
Bunny Rabbit Rolls, 116–17
Cauliflower Mac-'n'-Cheese Bites, 260–61
Cherry Tomato Cheddar Bites, 105
Creamy Asparagus Dip with Flax Crackers, 58–59
Feta-Cucumber Dip, 144–45
Grilled Cheddar and Pear Panini Sticks, 174–75
Kale Bread Pudding Bites, 254–55
kale pesto, 76–77
Mini Roasted Broccoli Pizzas, 246–47
Roasted Acorn Squash Quesadillas on Flour Tortillas, 222–23
Spinach and Ricotta Egg Muffin Cups, 172–73
Spinach Puffs, 72–73
Twice-Baked Mini Red Potatoes, 74–75
Yellow Cherry Tomato and Fresh Mozzarella Pesto Bites, 118–19
Zucchini and Squash Wheels with Marinara Dipping Sauce, 126–27
cherries
Cherry, Coconut, and Walnut Bread, 80–81
Cherry Chocolate Pudding Pops, 50–51
Cherry Coconut Lime Flavored Ice, 82–83
health benefits, 45, 83, 227
Jewel Mix, 227
Yogurt Granola Cups with Homemade Cherry Sauce, 44–45
chia seeds
as an ingredient, 33
Winter Granola, 236–37
chickpeas
Crispy Roasted Chickpeas, 234
health benefits, 235
Roasted Pumpkin Hummus, 170–71
chocolate, cocoa
Beet-Chocolate-Walnut Cookies, 180–81
Cherry Chocolate Pudding Pops, 50–51
Dark-Chocolate-Dipped Coconut Macaroons, 248–49
health benefits, 229
Hot Chocolate with Whipped Coconut Cream, 228–29
Jewel Mix, 227
cilantro
Black Bean Cakes, 136–37
Fresh Summer Rolls with Peanut Dipping Sauce, 140–41
Green Waffles, 70–71
Grilled Corn on the Cob with Lime Butter, 102–3
Raspberry Guacamole, 89
Vegetable Dumplings, 230–31
Clean Fifteen produce items, 10–11
coconut
Cherry, Coconut, and Walnut Bread, 80–81
Cherry Coconut Lime Flavored Ice, 82–83
Cranberry Granola Bars, 186–87
Dark-Chocolate-Dipped Coconut Macaroons, 248–49
Grilled Nectarine Skewers with Toasted Coconut, 142–43
health benefits, 187, 239
Heat Wave Pops, 123
Hot Chocolate with Whipped Coconut Cream, 228–29
as an ingredient, 30, 33
Sesame Seed Candy, 238–39
Winter Granola, 236–37

Yogurt-Dipped Dried Fruit, 244–45
coconut milk
Cherry Chocolate Pudding Pops, 50–51
Cherry Coconut Lime Flavored Ice, 82–83
Dark-Chocolate-Dipped Coconut Macaroons, 248–49
Fresh Summer Rolls with Peanut Dipping Sauce, 140–41
Green Smoothie Pops, 104
health benefits, 51
Maple Brown Rice Pudding, 216–17
coconut oil
Beet-Chocolate-Walnut Cookies, 180–81
Cranberry Gingerbread Cookies, 250–51
Dark-Chocolate-Dipped Coconut Macaroons, 248–49
flour tortillas, 116–17, 222–23
as an ingredient, 35
Lemon-Glazed Blueberry Donuts, 148–49
Oatmeal-Raisin Cookie Dough Balls, 242–43
Superfood Popcorn, 176–77
Winter Granola, 236–37
coconut sugar
Cranberry Granola Bars, 186–87
as an ingredient, 31
Mini Sweet Potato Pies, 258–59
cookies
Beet-Chocolate-Walnut Cookies, 180–81
Carrot Cake Sandwich Cookies, 184–85
Cranberry Gingerbread Cookies, 250–51
Cranberry Granola Bars, 186–87
Dark-Chocolate-Dipped Coconut Macaroons, 248–49
Oatmeal-Raisin Cookie Dough Balls, 242–43
Rhubarb-Lemon Biscotti, 94–95
Strawberry Frozen Yogurt Sandwiches, 52–53
corn
Black Bean Cakes, 136–37
Grilled Corn on the Cob with Lime Butter, 102–3
health benefits, 101, 103
Summer Corn Fritters, 100–101
Superfood Popcorn, 176–77
cornmeal
as an ingredient, 28
Sweet Potato–Cornmeal Muffins, 240–41
cranberries
Cranberry Gingerbread Cookies, 250–51
Cranberry Granola Bars, 186–87
Cranberry-Orange Buttermilk Snacking Cake, 154–55
health benefits, 155
Homemade Dried Cranberries on Sunflower Seed Butter Logs, 190–91
Winter Granola, 236–37
CSAs (community-supported agriculture), 9
cucumbers
Bunny Rabbit Rolls, 116–17
Feta-Cucumber Dip, 144–45
health benefits, 145

dairy farm, field trip to, 54
dates
Cranberry Granola Bars, 186–87
Eggnog Smoothie, 212–13
Oatmeal-Raisin Cookie Dough Balls, 242–43
date sugar
Cinnamon and Date Sugar Almonds, 210–11
Cranberry Granola Bars, 186–87
as an ingredient, 31
Mini Sweet Potato Pies, 258–59
dips, sauces, spreads
Baba Ghanoush, 138–39
basil pesto, 118–19
Carrot Miso Ginger Spread, 252–53
cherry sauce, 44–45
creamy asparagus dip, 58
Feta-Cucumber Dip, 144–45
honey-apricot glaze, 128–29
honey-mustard dip, 90
kale pesto, 76–77
lemony yogurt, 114–15
lime butter, for grilled corn, 102–3
Maple Almond Butter, 199
peanut sauce, for summer rolls, 141
Pear Sauce, 195
raspberry sauce, 60–61
Raspberry Guacamole, 89
Roasted Pumpkin Hummus, 170–71
soy-honey sauce, for dumplings, 230–31
for vegetable dipping bar, 46
whipped honey butter, for scones, 86–87
White Bean and Cauliflower Dip, 168–69
yogurt, for leek fritters, 66
yogurt-dill sauce, 220
Dirty Dozen produce items, 10–11
donuts, lemon-glazed blueberry, 148–49

eggplant
Baba Ghanoush, 138–39
health benefits, 139
eggs
Hard-Boiled Eggs with Kale Pesto, 76–77
health benefits, 173
Ratatouille Baked Egg Cups, 62–63
Spinach and Ricotta Egg Muffin Cups, 172–73

farmers' markets, 97, 151, 207
farms, field trips to
at harvest time, 158, 218
dairy, 54
pick your own, 112
flaxseed
Blueberry Baked Oatmeal Cups, 110–11
flax crackers, 58–59
health benefits, 59, 203
Honey-Wheat Bread, 202–3
Winter Granola, 236–37
flour, unbleached all-purpose, as an ingredient, 29
flour, whole wheat
Carrot-Apple Cinnamon Sticks, 192–93

flour, whole wheat (*continued*)
Cranberry-Orange Buttermilk Snacking Cake, 154–55
Honey-Wheat Bread, 202–3
as an ingredient, 30
Peach Olive Oil Muffins, 130–31
Raspberry-Lemon Whole Wheat Mini Pancakes, 134–35
Strawberry Rhubarb Crumb Muffins, 64–65
Sweet Potato–Cornmeal Muffins, 240–41
food preparation
in advance, 15
and being organized, 15–16
involving children in, 1, 17–19
packing and storage tips, 21–25
pantries, 16
food processor, 19
food shopping
buying in bulk, 8
buying locally, 7–8
joining a CSA, 9
organic foods, 9
preserving seasonal produce, 9
shopping lists, 14–15
time-saving techniques, 16–17
using seasonal ingredients, 5–7
French toast, 60–61
fritters
Leek Fritters, 66
Summer Corn Fritters, 100–101
frozen treats
Cherry Chocolate Pudding Pops, 50–51
Cherry Coconut Lime Flavored Ice, 82–83
Green Smoothie Pops, 104
Heat Wave Pops, 123
Honey Frozen Yogurt–Dipped Strawberries, 49
Melon Slushies, 106
Peach Frozen Yogurt, 108–9
pomegranate ice, 214–15
Strawberry Frozen Yogurt Sandwiches, 52–53
fruits, dried
Baked Apple Chips, 165
Carrot Cake Sandwich Cookies, 184–85
Cranberry Gingerbread Cookies, 250–51
Cranberry Granola Bars, 186–87
homemade dried cranberries, 190–91
as an ingredient, 31
Jewel Mix, 227
Oatmeal-Raisin Cookie Dough Balls, 242–43
Oven-Dried Stone Fruit, 124
Winter Granola, 236–37
Yogurt-Dipped Dried Fruit, 244–45
Zucchini Bread with Honey-Apricot Glaze, 128–29

ginger
Carrot-Apple Cinnamon Sticks, 192–93
Carrot Apple Ginger Juice, 166–67
Carrot Miso Ginger Spread, 252–53
Cranberry Gingerbread Cookies, 250–51
Crispy Roasted Chickpeas, 234
Grapefruit Ginger Juice with Pomegranate Ice, 214–15
health benefits, 166, 253
Roasted Sesame Peas, 57
Strawberry Rhubarb Crumb Muffins, 64–65
Vegetable Dumplings, 230–31
granola
Cranberry Granola Bars, 186–87
Winter Granola, 236–37
Yogurt Granola Cups with Homemade Cherry Sauce, 44–45
grapefruit
Grapefruit Ginger Juice with Pomegranate Ice, 214–15
health benefits, 215
green beans
Grilled Green Beans with Lemony Yogurt Dipping Sauce, 114–15
health benefits, 115

honey
Berry and Cream Scones with Whipped Honey Butter, 86–87
Carrot-Apple Cinnamon Sticks, 192–93
Carrot Cake Sandwich Cookies, 184–85
Cherry Chocolate Pudding Pops, 50–51
Cherry Coconut Lime Flavored Ice, 82–83
Eggnog Smoothie, 212–13
Grapefruit Ginger Juice with Pomegranate Ice, 214–15
Grilled Cheddar and Pear Panini Sticks, 174–75
Grilled Nectarine Skewers with Toasted Coconut, 142–43
Honey Frozen Yogurt–Dipped Strawberries, 49
Honey-Wheat Bread, 202–3
as an ingredient, 31
Raspberry French Toast Sticks, 60–61
Roasted Sesame Peas, 57
Sesame Seed Candy, 238–39
Spring Vegetable Spears with Dipping Bar, 46–47
Strawberry Frozen Yogurt Sandwiches, 52–53
Sugar Snap Peas with Honey-Mustard Dip, 90
Tomato-Scallion Biscuits, 146–47
Yogurt-Granola Cups with Homemade Cherry Sauce, 44–45
Zucchini Bread with Honey-Apricot Glaze, 128–29
hummus, roasted pumpkin, 170–71

ice cream maker, 19

kale
Green Smoothie Pops, 104
Hard-Boiled Eggs with Kale Pesto, 76–77
health benefits, 77, 104, 163, 255
Kale Bread Pudding Bites, 254–55
Kale Chips with Butternut Squash Seed Oil and Sea Salt, 162–63
kitchen appliances and supplies, recommended, 19–20

leeks
health benefits, 67
Leek Fritters, 66
lemons
Brussels Sprout Crisps with Parmesan and Lemon, 160–61
Grilled Green Beans with Lemony Yogurt Dipping Sauce, 114–15
health benefits, 121
Lemon-Glazed Blueberry Donuts, 148–49
Raspberry Lemonade, 120–21
Raspberry-Lemon Whole Wheat Mini Pancakes, 134–35
Rhubarb-Lemon Biscotti, 94–95
lime
Cherry Coconut Lime Flavored Ice, 82–83
Grapefruit Ginger Juice with Pomegranate Ice, 214–15
Green Waffles, 70–71
Grilled Corn on the Cob with Lime Butter, 102–3
Melon Slushies, 106
Raspberry Guacamole, 89

mangoes, 89
Green Smoothie Pops, 104
Yogurt-Dipped Dried Fruit, 244–45
maple syrup
Blueberry Baked Oatmeal Cups, 110–11
Carrot Cake Sandwich Cookies, 184–85
Cinnamon and Maple Roasted Pumpkin Seeds, 182–83
health benefits, 217
as an ingredient, 32
Maple Almond Butter, 199
Maple Brown Rice Pudding, 216–17
Mini Sweet Potato Pies, 259
Oatmeal-Raisin Cookie Dough Balls, 242–43
Peach Olive Oil Muffins, 130–31
Sesame Seed Candy, 238–39
Strawberry Rhubarb Crumb Muffins, 64–65
sugar house field trip, 218
Sweet Potato–Cornmeal Muffins, 240–41
Winter Granola, 236–37
Yogurt-Dipped Dried Fruit, 244–45
melon
health benefits, 106
Melon Slushies, 106
menu planning, 13–14
millet
Black Bean Cakes, 136–37
as an ingredient, 28
miso paste, Carrot Miso Ginger Spread, 252–53
molasses
Cranberry Gingerbread Cookies, 250–51
health benefits, 251
Sesame Seed Candy, 238–39
muffins, biscuits, scones
Berry and Cream Scones with Whipped Honey Butter, 86–87
Blueberry Baked Oatmeal Cups, 110–11
Peach Olive Oil Muffins, 130–31
Spinach and Ricotta Egg Muffin Cups, 172–73
Strawberry Rhubarb Crumb Muffins, 64
Sweet Potato–Cornmeal Muffins, 240–41
Tomato-Scallion Biscuits, 146–47
mushrooms, in vegetable dumplings, 230–31
mustard, in honey-mustard dip, 90

nectarines
Grilled Nectarine Skewers with Toasted Coconut, 142–43
health benefits, 143
Oven-Dried Stone Fruit, 124
nori
health benefits, 233
Sweet Potato–Quinoa Nori Rolls, 232–33
nut butters
as spreads and dips, 46–47
Winter Granola, 236–37
See also specific nuts
nuts, assorted, Jewel Mix, 227

oats, rolled
Blueberry Baked Oatmeal Cups, 110–11
Carrot-Apple Cinnamon Sticks, 192–93
Cranberry Granola Bars, 186–87
health benefits, 242–43
as an ingredient, 29
Oatmeal-Raisin Cookie Dough Balls, 242–43
Winter Granola, 236–37
olive oil, extra virgin
basil pesto, 118–19
health benefits, 131
as an ingredient, 35
kale pesto, 76–77
Peach Olive Oil Muffins, 130–31
Zucchini Bread with Honey-Apricot Glaze, 128–29
oranges, orange juice
Berry and Cream Scones with Whipped Honey Butter, 86–87
Butternut Squash Turnovers, 256–57
Cranberry-Orange Buttermilk Snacking Cake, 154–55
Green Smoothie Pops, 104
Pea-Avocado Smoothie, 93
organic foods, 9

packing and storing food, 21–25
pancakes, lemon-raspberry, 134–35
parsnip, in crispy root vegetable patties, 220–21
pasta, for cauliflower mac'n'cheese, 260–61
peaches
health benefits, 124
Oven-Dried Stone Fruit, 124
Peach Frozen Yogurt, 108–9
Peach Olive Oil Muffins, 130–31
peanut butter
peanut dipping sauce, 141
Sesame Seed Candy, 238–39
pears
Grilled Cheddar and Pear Panini Sticks, 174–75

pears (*continued*)
health benefits, 175, 195
Pear Sauce, 195
peas
health benefits, 57, 90, 93
Pea-Avocado Smoothie, 93
Roasted Sesame Peas, 57
Sugar Snap Peas with Honey-Mustard Dip, 90
pecans
Carrot-Apple Cinnamon Sticks, 192–93
Cranberry Granola Bars, 186–87
as an ingredient, 33
Quinoa Pudding with Raspberries and Pecans, 84–85
peppers, red bell
Bunny Rabbit Rolls, 116–17
health benefits, 117
Ratatouille Baked Egg Cups, 62–63
Summer Corn Fritters, 100–101
pesto
Hard-Boiled Eggs with Kale Pesto, 76–77
Yellow Cherry Tomato and Fresh Mozzarella Pesto Bites, 118–19
phyllo dough, Spinach Puffs, 72–73
pie crust, 259
pies, sweet potato, 258–59
pine nuts
basil pesto, 118–19
as an ingredient, 33
kale pesto, 76–77
pistachio nuts
Dark-Chocolate-Dipped Coconut Macaroons, 248–49
health benefits, 249
as an ingredient, 33
pita bread
Apple Power Pockets, 179
White Bean and Cauliflower Dip with Baked Pita Chips, 169
pizza, pizza dough, 246–47
plant nursery, field trip to, 79
plums
health benefits, 245
Oven-Dried Stone Fruit, 124
pomegranate ice, 214–15
potatoes
health benefits, 75, 225
Oven-Baked French Fries, 224–25
Twice-Baked Mini Red Potatoes, 74–75
produce
Dirty Dozen and Clean Fifteen, 10–11
fall favorites, 152
grow-your-own, 9
seasonal, benefits of using, 5–7
seasonal, preserving, 9
spring favorites, 41
summer favorites, 99
winter favorites, 209
puff pastry, Butternut Squash Turnovers, 256–57
pumpkin
health benefits, 171, 183
Roasted Pumpkin Hummus, 170–71
pumpkin seeds
Cinnamon and Maple Roasted Pumpkin Seeds, 182–83
as an ingredient, 34
Winter Granola, 236–37

quinoa
health benefits, 85
as an ingredient, 29
Quinoa Pudding with Raspberries and Pecans, 84–85
Sweet Potato–Quinoa Nori Rolls, 232–33

radishes
health benefits, 47
Spring Vegetable Spears with Dipping Bar, 46–47
raisins
Carrot-Apple Cinnamon Sticks, 192–93
Carrot Cake Sandwich Cookies, 184–85
Jewel Mix, 227
Oatmeal-Raisin Cookie Dough Balls, 242–43
Zucchini Bread with Honey-Apricot Glaze, 128–29
raspberries
health benefits, 61, 135
Heat Wave Pops, 123
Quinoa Pudding with Raspberries and Pecans, 84–85
Raspberry French Toast Sticks, 60–61
Raspberry Guacamole, 89
Raspberry Lemonade, 120–21
Raspberry-Lemon Whole Wheat Mini Pancakes, 134–35
rhubarb
health benefits, 65, 95
Rhubarb-Lemon Biscotti, 94–95
Strawberry Rhubarb Crumb Muffins, 64
rice
as an ingredient, 29
Maple Brown Rice Pudding, 216–17
rice vinegar, 252–53

sauces. *See* dips, sauces, spreads
scallions
Fresh Summer Rolls with Peanut Dipping Sauce, 140–41
Green Waffles, 70–71
health benefits, 71
Tomato-Scallion Biscuits, 146–47
Vegetable Dumplings, 230–31
scones, 86–87
seed butters, 46–47
Sesame Seed Candy, 238–39
Winter Granola, 236–37
See also specific seeds
seeds, assorted, Jewel Mix, 227
sesame oil
Carrot Miso Ginger Spread, 252–53
as an ingredient, 35
Vegetable Dumplings, 230–31
sesame seeds
Carrot Miso Ginger Spread, 252–53
as an ingredient, 34
Roasted Sesame Peas, 57
Sesame Seed Candy, 238–39
skillet, cast iron, 19
slushies, melon, 106

smoothies
Eggnog Smoothie, 212–13
Green Smoothie Pops, 104
Pea-Avocado Smoothie, 93
Purple Panda Smoothie, 200–201
spelt flour
as an ingredient, 29
Rhubarb-Lemon Biscotti, 94–95
spinach
Bunny Rabbit Rolls, 116–17
Green Waffles, 70–71
health benefits, 73, 201
Purple Panda Smoothie, 200–201
Spinach and Ricotta Egg Muffin Cups, 172–73
Spinach Puffs, 72–73
spirulina
health benefits, 177
Superfood Popcorn, 176–77
spreads. *See* dips, sauces, spreads
spring rolls, 140–41
squash, summer
Zucchini and Squash Wheels with Marinara Dipping Sauce, 126–27
See also zucchini
squash, winter
Butternut Squash Turnovers, 256–57
health benefits, 223, 257
Kale Chips with Butternut Squash Seed Oil and Sea Salt, 162–63
oil from, as an ingredient, 34–35
Roasted Acorn Squash Quesadillas on Flour Tortillas, 222–23
storing food, containers for, 21–25
strawberries
Berry and Cream Scones with Whipped Honey Butter, 86–87
health benefits, 49, 69
Honey Frozen Yogurt–Dipped Strawberries, 49
Strawberry Frozen Yogurt Sandwiches, 52–53
Strawberry Fruit Leather, 66–67
Strawberry Rhubarb Crumb Muffins, 64
sugar, as an ingredient, 30–32
sunflower seeds
Bunny Rabbit Rolls, 116–17
health benefits, 191
Homemade Dried Cranberries on Sunflower Seed Butter Logs, 190–91
as an ingredient, 34
Sesame Seed Candy, 238–39
Spring Vegetable Spears with Dipping Bar, 46–47
Sweet Potato–Cornmeal Muffins, 240–41
Winter Granola, 236–37
Yogurt-Dipped Dried Fruit, 244–45
sweet potato
health benefits, 241, 259
Mini Sweet Potato Pies, 258–59
Sweet Potato–Cornmeal Muffins, 240–41
Sweet Potato–Quinoa Nori Rolls, 232–33

tahini
Baba Ghanoush, 138–39
as an ingredient, 34
Sesame Seed Candy, 238–39
tomatoes
Cherry Tomato Cheddar Bites, 105
health benefits, 105, 147
Mini Roasted Broccoli Pizzas, 246–47
Ratatouille Baked Egg Cups, 62–63
Tomato-Scallion Biscuits, 146–47
Yellow Cherry Tomato and Fresh Mozzarella Pesto Bites, 118–19
tortillas, flour
Bunny Rabbit Rolls, 116–17
homemade, 222–23
Roasted Acorn Squash Quesadillas on Flour Tortillas, 222–23

waffles, 70–71
walnuts
Beet-Chocolate-Walnut Cookies, 180–81
Carrot Cake Sandwich Cookies, 184–85
Cherry, Coconut, and Walnut Bread, 80–81
Creamy Asparagus Dip with Flax Crackers, 58–59
health benefits, 81, 185
as an ingredient, 34
Jewel Mix, 227
Strawberry Rhubarb Crumb Muffins, 64–65
Zucchini Bread with Honey-Apricot Glaze, 128–29
wheat germ
Cranberry Granola Bars, 186–87
Honey-Wheat Bread, 202–3
as an ingredient, 29
Raspberry-Lemon Whole Wheat Mini Pancakes, 134–35
Sesame Seed Candy, 238–39

yeast, nutritional, with popcorn, 176–77
yogurt
Blueberry Lassi, 133
Crispy Root Vegetable Patties with Yogurt-Dill Sauce, 220–21
Eggnog Smoothie, 212–13
Feta-Cucumber Dip, 144–45
Grilled Green Beans with Lemony Yogurt Dipping Sauce, 114–15
health benefits, 53, 109, 213
Honey Frozen Yogurt–Dipped Strawberries, 49
Leek Fritters, 66–67
Peach Frozen Yogurt, 108–9
Roasted Pumpkin Hummus, 170–71
Strawberry Frozen Yogurt Sandwiches, 52–53
Strawberry Rhubarb Crumb Muffins, 64–65
Sugar Snap Peas with Honey-Mustard Dip, 90
Yogurt-Dipped Dried Fruit, 244–45
Yogurt Granola Cups with Homemade Cherry Sauce, 44–45

zucchini
health benefits, 63, 127
Ratatouille Baked Egg Cups, 62–63
Zucchini and Squash Wheels with Marinara Dipping Sauce, 126–27
Zucchini Bread with Honey-Apricot Glaze, 128–29

About Us

CHRISTINE CHITNIS is a writer, photographer, mother, and home cook. She lives with her husband and two young sons in Providence, Rhode Island. Her writing and photography are inspired by the farmland and coasts of her adopted home state, though her love of the natural world dates back to childhood summers spent in Northern Michigan. Her writing has appeared in *Country Living*, the *Boston Globe*, and *Edible Rhody*, among many other local and national publications. Christine's first book, *Markets of New England* (The Little Bookroom 2011), highlights fifty of the most unique and vibrant farmers' markets and art events in the region. For adventures in cooking, gardening, mothering, and crafting visit ChristineChitnis.com.

SARAH WALDMAN is a home cook, certified health counselor, recipe developer, and mother. She lives with her husband and two young sons on Martha's Vineyard. While pregnant with her first son, she attended the Institute of Integrative Nutrition, acting on her urge to stop the cycle of processed and low-quality food appearing on America's dinner tables. Follow Sarah's island adventures in cooking local, seasonal, wholesome family food at SarahWaldman.com.